THE
INVENTION
OF THE
NEGRO

BOOKS BY EARL CONRAD

Harriet Tubman
Jim Crow America
Scottsboro Boy (*with Haywood Patterson*)
The Public School Scandal
Rock Bottom
Horse Trader
Gulf Stream North
News of the Nation (*Co-author*)
Mr. Seward for the Defense
The Governor and His Lady
Crane Eden
The Premier
The Ecstasy Machine:
    Tales of the Population Explosion
The Invention of the Negro

THE
INVENTION
OF THE
NEGRO

by

EARL CONRAD

PAUL S. ERIKSSON, INC.

New York

FOR ALYSE

Who Has Been With Me Throughout
With Thanks and Acknowledgment
And Love

TABLE OF CONTENTS

FOREWORD

"It is a tremendous task," writes Gunnar Myrdal in *The American Dilemma,* "for theoretical research to find out why the Negro's status is what it is."

In this single sentence Myrdal points to the heart of the basic issue involving the Negro people in America in the second half of the twentieth century: Who and what brought the Negro to the second-class status against which he struggles today?

Unfortunately, like so many other books in this field, *The American Dilemma,* having raised the one supremely cogent question, then procedes to bypass it in favor of examining once again the various aspects of Negro life in America quite apart from how these cultural patterns and phenomena came into being and how they persist to this day.

In this present work I have sought by wholly different social and historical avenues from those of the past to probe this question of the how and the why. I have sought out these new routes in the unshakable conviction that the questions involved here cannot be and never could be answered merely by examining the Negro himself, his ghettos, his history, his personality, his culture. For the answer to how the Negro's status came to be what it is does not lie essentially in the world of the Negro, but in the world of the white.

It will be found not in an examination and evaluation of Negro patterns but of so-called white institutions, white history; in the statements not of Negro but of white European and American leadership, both religious and political; in white concepts, white commerce and white self-deception, from the days of Columbus and earlier down to the present.

This book is therefore a look at history specifically as it relates to what the white man—English, European, and above all the American—has done or failed to do for his Negro brother.

A large portion of the white world has preferred for centuries to overlook this perspective; it may well be uncomfortable for our collective conscience. Yet it is a vital and essential one to explore if we are to grasp at last what we of the white world have done to bring about the present perilous period of racial turbulence and crisis in America.

So in this work I have undertaken a special task: to describe how and by what means the white overworld designed, shaped and indeed invented the Negro in the image and likeness of a second-class human being.

E.C.

One night in 1964 when the civil rights rising was high in the nation James Baldwin was on television talking to the white world. His angry eyes stared into a nation of white viewers. Without blinking he said to each white who viewed him, "If I am a nigger you invented me."

This is the story of that invention.

OUT OF AFRICA

Fifty years before Columbus sailed westward, Catholic Spain and Catholic Portugal were engaged in a rivalry to sack Africa, to seize its inhabitants as slaves and to ship them back to Europe and sell them. Portugal, the first invader, sought and secured the blessing of the Popes and in a series of papal bulls issued from 1443 on there is the spectacle of the Christian Vatican sanctifying the enslavement of Africans on grounds that they were pagans —and winking its eye at the profit in the trade.

Prince Henry of Portugal, claiming that he was a missionary bent upon saving the souls of the Africans, took the Africans as "souls" and sold them as slaves in the ports of Portugal. He asked absolution for the seamen taking part in the voyages, and Pope Eugenia IV in 1442, for one, granted the request. By 1452 Pope Nicholas V gave to King Alfonso of Spain general powers to enslave "pagans." Pagans meant the Africans who didn't yet know Christ.

So controlling was the power of the Vatican in the conduct of trade into Africa that in 1481 Edward IV of England asked the Pope for permission to trade in Africa.

After a time, and because of the increasing competition from a half dozen countries to secure a foothold in Africa, papal bulls lost their effect—and there was open warfare for control of the slave trade into Africa by a half dozen European countries. By 1600 there was often little pretense about proselytising. God's work be damned, make the money, said the traders of Portugal, Spain, France, Holland and England.

Moreover, a hint of the destiny of the African as a slave—and later on as ex-slave rising to second-class citizenship status—was prophesied by the intentions of Christopher Columbus. He beheld the Indians as a slave supply, for he wrote in 1493 to Spain asking for help and promised in return the riches of the New World, "and slaves, as many as they shall order, who will be idolaters." Apparently he held it legitimate to enslave the New World natives as long as they weren't Christians. But it did not take long for the emphasis to shift to the African, already a servant in Europe, and later transported annually to New World slavery by the thousands.

For the next two hundred years, as the Americas, North and South, began filling with slaves, contending European nations met with no admonitions from the Papacy against slavery. On the contrary, they were given the utmost cooperation. In Spain, the Council of the Indies and the Council of the Inquisition pressed the trade in humans and whenever these ruling bodies were in difficulties with other nations they hastened to the Vatican where they found judgment and decisions forwarding their interest. No questions of conscience were offered by the Popes when there was an issue of intensifying Catholic positions in "the Indies" as the New World continents were called. The Council of the Indies told His Majesty, the King of Spain, in July 1685, that there was no alternative to the introduction of slavery into the New World if these lands were to thrive. It was now "the general custom in the kingdoms of Castile, America, and Portugal, without any objection on the part of His Holiness or ecclesiastical state, but rather with the tolerance of all of them."

Marco Polo had made his voyage East, still fifty years before Columbus would move westward with the *Nina,* the *Pinta* and the *Santa Maria.* Yet a small incident on the Coast of Guinea more than five hundred and fifty years ago may have been as significant as those events.

Gomes Eannes de Azurara, royal librarian and keeper

of the archives of Portugal, was with a company of explorers, soldiers and adventurers led by an illustrious man, The Infant, representative of the Pope. They were on a stony shore beneath hot sun, palms surrounded them and a coastal breeze blew softly. The Portuguese had fallen into possession of several hundred black-skinned captives who were about to be distributed in shares to the soldiery. Whole families of men, women and children, naked, huddled together and bound by chains, stood in the center. Other Africans who had taken them in war were behind them: before them were the Portuguese who had secured them in trade from an African Chief for a few cents worth of European-made baubles.

The archivist Azurara, recórding all this on the scene, was deeply moved. He saw how the black families were being broken up. He observed that they were human beings. He broke into tears of pity. It occurred to him that if brute animals, dogs, cats and snakes, with even their bestial feelings by a natural instinct understood the sufferings of their own kind, ". . . what wouldst Thou have my human nature to do on seeing before my eyes that miserable company, and remembering that they too are of the generation of Adam?"

Azurara looked to God for a moment, through his weeping. Then he beheld the Papal representative, mounted upon his powerful steed, his retinue around him. He saw him as a generous man, making distribution of his favors as one who sought to gain but small treasure from his legal share. Of the forty-six souls that fell to the Papal emissary as his fifth, or share, wrote Azurara, he made a very speedy partition of these; his chief riches lay in the accomplishment of his purpose: the salvation of these souls that before were lost.

Once more Azurara prayed to God, and later, in

1533, he would write in his *Chronicle of the Discovery and Conquest of Guinea:* "O powerful Fortune . . . put before the eyes of that miserable people some understanding of matters to come, that they may receive some consolation in the midst of their great sorrow."

And, thought the archivist, as he glanced again at The Infant on the powerful steed: "And you who are so busy in making the division of the captives, look with pity upon so much misery; and see how they cling to one another, so that you can hardly separate them."

So came the Europeans, so they conquered: so, in the name of God, the church and the Pope made they their earliest divisions of human personnel; so began the most numerous and barbaric enslaving in the annals of man; so began the invention of new human moralities and immoralities; so was unearthed and formed the black human lever which would, in large part, pry and uproot and build the New World; so began, in prayers to God and a turning away from God, that debasement of values and ideals which led to the invention of the modern American Negro and to so much of the shaping of a modern universal race concept.

It was possible for Europe to seize Africa, to plunder it and enslave its peoples, for only one overriding reason: the Africans were neither organized nor unified.

Africa may have been organized by state, tribe or family-tribal arrangements sufficiently for intra-continental survival, but even that is doubtful. The varie-gated communities with their various forms of life, hundreds of differing tribal segments in all sections of the large continent, formed a land of anarchic social systems, of numerous languages, of hunting tribes and farming peoples and vast distance barriers of mountain, river and forest. All of this organically restrained the separate peoples into island-like communities and prevented even the thought of a continental force and unity.

The broadest vision was the nation-state concept of some sizeable kingdoms, mostly in the Sudan, and this until the 1500's may have been sufficient for intracontinental survival of the mass of Africans. Conquest from and by outsiders until then was not a sufficient threat to bring about unified thinking, outlook or defense.

This split-up into large kingdoms, lesser kingdoms, small provinces, tribal and familial arrangements made it possible for Africa to be plundered from within and seized from without.

Whites supremacist concepts of contemporary times began in that period when European national collisions occurred in a struggle for Africa, and when Africa and its people became economic factors in Europe's conquest of the Western Hemisphere.

Few European peoples were exempt from their violent part: the Dutch, the Dane, the Swede, Brandenburger, French, Portuguese, English, all were involved. The well-to-do of Europe helped finance slave ships and dragged in the trapped or desperate or adventurous as hired hands to do work, the actual commerce and physical business of enslavement.

All of Europe had a hand in ravaging Africa, in despoiling its inhabitants, and in helping to blot out its thousands of years of history and culture. Black men and women were brought into each of these countries, though in small numbers, and with their presence came tales of the defenseless continent from which they had been stolen. Europe for centuries was infused in a thousand ways with knowledge of a continent of people below, with whom there was little or no communication, only war and death; they were a defenseless people; they could be made to work if chained. So the Europeans thrust southward into that peopled, ancient Africa which had been known and noted thousands of years earlier even by the Old Testament's Isaiah (18:1) who remarked ". . . the land shadowing with wings which is beyond the rivers of Ethiopia."

The Factory or Fort on the Gold Coast, where slaves were bought and sold, was the original source of the split between white and black humanity, the cellular origin of the color line, the beginning of white supremacy which today haunts the American scene. These Factories, existing for centuries, were run by European business men called Factors. But the word Factory was in large measure a misnomer. These business camps, so-called, were prisons, internment centers, training camps for the preparation of slaves for labor on foreign soil.

"Racial" origin, as we know it now, pre-formed embryonically at these Factory Forts along three thousand miles of the upper Western African Coast where the bulge and the inward curve occur. The condition was war. War changes minds, attitudes and ways. African tribes, warring upon one another, took slaves, transported them to the coast, sold them to the European traders who conducted an exchange of goods for slaves at these Forts. War, kidnaping, capture, enslavement, force: these were the ingredients of the earliest mind-changing events. That was the gestation period.

The Forts were combination mercantile and military centers where Portuguese, Dutch, English, French, Danes and others established their control by means of arms and arrogance, cruelty and indifference. Though the Portuguese dominated the slave trade for a century, from about 1550 to 1650, other European nations from the earliest days tried to make inroads into Africa, and by the mid-1700s the English took over the trade and dominated it for the remainder of its existence.

The Cabo Corso Castle, owned by a British group called the Royal African Company, was a fortification of outworks, platforms and bastions, built of brick, lime and a product called tarras. The structure took seven years to complete.

In one part of the Fort were apartments for a Director General, Factors (traders), writers, mechanics and soldiers. Other sections were given over to arms magazines. There were warehouses, storehouses, granaries, guard rooms. To feed and house slaves and operators there were two large water tanks or cisterns built of brick and tarras brought in from England. These cisterns were so huge they could contain two hundred tons of water. They had a polite name for the pens, cells or blocks which contained the slaves: repositories. There were vaults for rum and workhouses for smiths and carpenters. The structure was defended by seventy-four great guns, by small arms, blunderbusses, bucanneer guns, pistols, cartouche boxes, swords and cutlasses. One block house contained ammunition for great guns and small arms. There were sections with stores and tools for bricklayers, brickmakers, armorers, gunners and gardeners. Because religion was necessary to justify the role of Englishmen in the not-so-tender task of taking slaves, part of the bastion was a chapel. There were small boats for communication between slaveships offshore and the Fortress where business was transacted. Seamen, stevedores, messengers, workmen of all types passed between the slaveships and the Fort; the traffic flow was heavy.

The transformation of captured Africans from persons
with tribal cultures of their own into a new sub-order,
reshaped for service in the New World, began at once at
these Forts. A function of the Factories was the training
or seasoning of the captives as skilled and semi-skilled
workmen ready to enter into the process of building the
towns, cities and plantation properties of the Western
Hemisphere. Africans who may have been seized fifteen
hundred miles inland and taken from traditional occupations such as hunting or farming were instructed in what
the English called "the mechanic arts." They were prepared as smiths, carpenters, armorers, masons, stonecut-
ters, sawyers and brickmakers. When properly trained
they were worth a thousand pounds apiece.

It is in the light of this stark economic fact that we
must begin to consider how this "invention" with which
we are concerned here took root in our culture, found
acceptance and justification in the hearts and conscience
of our communities, our prelates, pastors and rabbis, our
cultural leaders. It is this economic base which com-
pels us today, as modern enlightened human beings, to
explore these tortuous roots across history, these causes,
the primordial roots of second-class citizenship.

Multiply the picture of Corbo Castle and the training
activity in that Fort by the industry going on in hundreds
of these Factories for four centuries and one can begin to
comprehend the dehumanizing crucible that took human
beings and transformed them into tools. These Forts
were maintained by the various European countries at
the public expense. The list of such centers was endless,
all set up more or less alike. Some had names reminiscent
of home: York, Williams, James, Bence Island; mostly
they had African names—Annisham, Agga, Tantum-
querry, Shidoe, Alamapo, Commenda, Annamaboe,
Winnebah, Accra.

The names are cited not to lend quaintness to any of it but rather to indicate the English-African spread and identification along this whole coast: for the only meaning of these cauldrons was death, starvation, whippings, revolt, bribery, suicides, escapes, disease.

The master-slave schism hardened in the phase known as the Middle Passage, the trip to the West Indies. Most of the slaveships were floating concentration camps and when they left the Gold Coast their captains were hopeful that at least half the human cargo would be alive upon arrival.

The human toll of African life in the several centuries of the slave trade, in the slave wars in Africa itself, in the entire colonial conquest of Africa, has been estimated at no less than fifty million lives. They lost their lives in an endless tide of resistance. Some of this massive fatality was from disease, hunger, and crushing physical and emotional impairment brought on by imprisonment and mistreatment. Most of the loss was in actual warfare: the black man's outweaponed struggle against his original enslavement, against the Factors and the Forts in which he was held, against the ships' captains and their crews on the Middle Passage, and later against their masters in the New World. Fifty million dead—some have estimated it as high as a hundred million—testified to the capacity for self-defense of the African. This was resistance of unprecedented order, a people struggling against a predatory enemy.

No record in the annals of man is more illustrative of the natural propensity toward self defense. Notably in that record of the journey from Africa to the West are the endless tales of whole cargoes of captives leaping overboard into the ocean, throwing their infants overboard; mass suicides, mutinies, fasting to death. They were beaten, killed and destroyed by plague—but always some survived.

Thomas Phillips commanded the *Hannibal,* a slaveship that traveled the Atlantic in the late 1600s. He was a thoughtful man who as a youth had been ambitious to acquire riches. Seeking his fortune, he went to sea, a young man, muscled, tall, with eyes blue as the sea he sailed. Learning the craft of the slavers, he soon became the commander of a bitter little ship destined to make scores of trips from the Gold Coast to the West Indies. He became older but not much richer for all his human cargo. But he did keep records and descriptions.

There was the time, these records disclose, when he started out from Africa with seven hundred slaves. En route, the smallpox swept the Africans and began to decimate them. The crew heaved them overboard. When the smallpox didn't carry them away a kind of distemper which they called the flux, probably dysentery, carried off other scores. And moaned he, all to his great regret and the regret of the sailors because care had been taken to give the captives their messes in due order and season and the ship's crew had tried to keep the lodgings as clean and sweet as possible, yet they had endured so much misery and stench among a parcel of creatures whom he described as being nastier than swine.

Captain Phillips was entirely candid about the affair. It certainly appeared, he confessed, that the great death rate was occasioned by the ship's being crowded and pestered with such an excess of slaves being taken aboard that they didn't really have the room to stow them.

No gold-finders could endure so much, he laments, as they did who carried Negroes: "For we endure twice the misery; and yet by their mortality our voyages are ruined, and we pine and fret ourselves to death, to think that we should undergo so much misery and take so much pains to so little purpose." To the company's Factors at Barbadoes he delivered alive only three hundred and seventy-two.

In the earliest days of the slave trade Africans were seized solely as economic units, a source of simple profit, at so much a head. With time it became necessary to work out a rationale, a sop to the moralistic for holding in captivity so much humanity, and it may have been a natural or logical or inevitable process that the slavers would hit upon color itself as a powerful lever. The annals of the slave trade do not often yield up such vivid keys to this as appeared in the instance of the experience of slavetrader William Snelgrave of Liverpool. He too had commanded ships in the late 1600s and into the 1700s and among the stories he told was that of the execution of an African who had slain a white crewman.

The African was captured and re-enchained and Snelgrave, through an interpreter, told him that he would die in an hour, for "you have killed a white man."

An interpreter repeated that to the African and the condemned man made reply: "If you do that you will lose all the money that you paid for me."

Snelgrave turned to the interpreter and said, "Tell him that I'll waive the profit in this case for the crime is that a black man has slain a white one."

The cargo of slaves was lined up to see the African hoisted to a yard-arm. Then Captain Snelgrave ordered ten white crewmen to take aim.

But before the captain ordered the fire he turned to the interpreter and he said, "Linguist, tell them that now they may judge, that no one who kills a white man shall be spared."

On board the slaveship *Zong,* Captain Andrew Lockwood called his officers and chief crewmen to his cabin. Addressing primarily his mate, Luke Collingswood, he said, "As you know we are insured against accidental death of the slaves. Many are sick. If they die of natural causes the owners of our ship in London can't collect. Now, Mister Collingswood, there is only one thing we can do. We have to throw these sick slaves into the sea. That way the underwriters will have to pay off." The mate and some of the others protested, but Captain Lockwood went into the economics. They would all lose their jobs when they returned if so many slaves died a natural death; but if they could report that there was a mutiny and in self-defense the mutineers were tossed overboard, they would be in the clear. That evening Luke Collingswood and his crew picked a hundred and thirty-three of the sick slaves, those most likely to die, and ordered them brought to the deck. The crew was then directed, by turns, to heave them into the ocean. ". . . which most inhuman order was cruelly complied with," as one witness put it.

Even these weakened slaves resisted and it wasn't easy drowning them. It became dark, began to rain, still the work of heaving the sick went on. By midnight it was done.

The incident came to light when it became an action at court back in England later when the insurers refused to pay the claim. The court in finding against the insurers, said the whole issue hinged on necessity, and had to be judged exactly as if they had thrown overboard a cargo of horses.

The Negro people's present struggle in America for a rightful place in today's world began with such unspeak able crimes, guilt and evil that cannot be shrugged away, even centuries later.

Yet even in those beginning days, despite the killings and cruelty of white traders against their Negro captives, the slave traffic is filled with the ingenuity, resourcefulness as well as the desperation of the enslaved. On board the *Prince of Orange,* at St. Christopher's in the West Indies early one evening—revolts often occurred at that time—a hundred men leaped overboard, resolved to die rather than be used in the West Indies as slaves. Crewmen saved about seventy, but thirty-three Negroes went down.

In another dramatic instance a distress gun boomed from an English slaver in the harbor of Guadaloupe. French and English ships raced to the side of the distressed ship. Crews of the assisting ships got on board the slaver to discover that slaves had leaped on the crew, killing and wounding many. One lone slave had fallen into possession of a hammer. With it he broke the shackles on himself and his comrades. But like many such risings it was abortive, and when it was over twenty slaves had lost their lives. Yet the slaves lived for the exhilarating moment when by one mischance or another they had the opportunity to mutiny.

There was widespread fear among the slaves that upon being landed in the New World they were to be eaten. Fear of being eaten made them desperate. On any ship where this fear ran high there was always a mutiny, no matter how abortive. On board the *Yorkshire,* the master had fished up an anchor of a departed English vessel and he put the anchor in the hold where the slaves were stowed. They smashed their fetters against the iron anchor and liberated themselves. They raced up on deck, cut the cook's throat, slashed the boatswain through his middle, cut several sailors to the bone, but all the time they were running about cutting up half of the crew the other crewmen fired on them, killing some and wounding others. Once more the most mutinous leaped into the ocean rather than undergo refettering.

It was the practice of many slavers to allow the women and children to move about freely on deck. But this often led to uprisings for the women found ways of helping their men. One ship's captain writing to another on how to run a slaver counseled in the language of that time "putt not too much confidence in the women nor the children least they happen to be instrumental to your being surprised which may be fatall."

So the slaves resisted. They pillaged vessels when they could do that; they murdered and cut up their oppressors when they had the opportunity. When they could do no other they leaped overboard to drown in the open sea. Sometimes they seized ships and tried to run them back to the African coast. Few succeeded.

The traffic grew with the profits—the shuttle service importing human chattel to America in overcrowded ships.

It was on these ships that we find the beginnings—the first crystalizations—of the curious doctrine which was to be called "white supremacy."

INTO THE NEW WORLD

Among the first white men to develop attitudes of supremacy were the slaveship crews. They were men of varied backgrounds: privateers, seamen, tailors, chaplains, carpenters, gunners, surgeons, cooks, stewards, skippers, mates, coopers, armorers, men of skills needed to keep a ship afloat and to guard and attend to human cargoes.

Forty-six crewmen shipped on board the *Sally,* a vessel which regularly left England for Africa and thence to the West Indies during the 1700s. A complicated contract bound the men and the owners, spelling out all the possibilities of incident, accident and responsibility that could occur in the dangerous work of slaving.

The contract stated that James Cross, the commander of the *Sally,* his officers and mariners, his seamen, landsmen and boys, would perform their services during the whole voyage "without any manner of Denial, Mutiny or Resistance whatsoever." Each and every one must perform the voyage honestly and faithfully and in no way embezzle the goods or the merchandise—the slaves. Nor could they steal the ship's stores. All must obey the Master of the ship and his orders.

But from the moment such ships left England, the crews and their officers were in trouble. Sometimes the men went without water or with small rations of it; their food was poor and often they were not paid; they had to put up with hard captains; their sleeping accommodations weren't much better than what the slaves had; and throughout the Middle Passage they lived in fear of black uprisings.

Faced with such conditions, the crewmen often entered into trading, bartering and thieving arrangements themselves, breaking away from their own ships, joining forces with competitors.

The slavetrading process was commercial war rather than routine commerce. The men who ran the ships were themselves castaways of the human species. Nineteen of the *Sally*'s crew signed their names with an X-mark. If they themselves didn't succeed in developing as tradesmen and leaders in the Gold Coast commerce, they tended to become part of the early mercenaries of the West.

Still, these unlettered, poorly paid, half-starved seamen found themselves in a position of feeling better off than the black men, women and children herded aboard. They had the relative freedom of the prison. That they were free, however, and of another culture and color, identified them with the whole movement of the conquerer, the master, the superior being, sorry specimens as they were.

Diseases that spread among the slaves—smallpox, dysentery and pellegra—carried away the young English and Irish sailors with steady regularity. The death rate became severe. In the time of Thomas Clarkson, a reform movement developed in England to look into their conditions, for it was perceived that this branch of the mercantile service had an excessive mortality rate.

So hardened did the slave ship crews become that out of their ranks came the earliest pirates. Poor pay and the toughening experience of handling slaves brutalised these men; it was no great step to plan the murder of the commanders and the seizure of the vessels. The English slaving tradition and the piracy tradition were concurrent; the one was an offshoot of the other.

Crews either seized ships abandoned at sea, or mutinied against captains. Sometimes they took over a ship that might be left on the Gold Coast after everybody on board, captain and all, was dead of a plague. Then a half dozen armed young men, usually in their twenties and thirties, seized the ship and made off to maraud their way from sea to sea, continent to continent.

The slave trade raging up and down three thousand miles of the African coast became the lifestream of European commerce. It involved directly and indirectly scores of millions of all of Europe, and it prospered England.

Apart from the crews on the slaveships, it took all kinds of vocationally trained persons to provide the paraphernalia to capture the Africans and to help maintain them on the colonial plantations. Equipping the Forts along the Gold Coast alone required large manufacture in England.

Workingmen who were engaged in every kind of productivity in England, France, Germany and Portugal depended upon export of the articles they made for their livelihood. Items of all variety went into the exchange processes by which blacks were made captive. This exchange of men for baubles bred a callousness toward the African in the mind of the European worker. It led to that tolerance of colonial conquest which was to persist in European peoples.

English labor, engaged in making knickknacks, baubles, gunpowder and shipping materials for use in subduing the Africans, fought for a continuance of the traffic.

When in 1708 there was an issue in England over the Royal African Company, many workingmen leaped to the support of the Crown-sponsored company, and asked the House of Commons to do all in its power to protect it. Gunmakers, cutlers and powder-makers of London petitioned the House, asking that the traffic of the Royal African Company be preserved and encouraged because, they said, their families were supported by sale of their goods. Dyers, packers, setters, drawers and calenders addressed themselves to the House saying that their families had been supported by the working and fitting for sale of woolen manufactures, and a decline in the slave traffic would be the complete ruin of many of them. The same

with shipwrights, sail-makers, rope-makers and other
tradesmen involved in shipping; also weavers, tuckers,
and other artificers, as the petition put it, engaged in the
making of wearing apparel called perpetuanoes for
Africa. Workmen in Liverpool, Birmingham, Exom and
elsewhere, engaged in wrought iron and textile manufacture, protested to London.

Whatever went on in the colonies to hold the ex-
African to the plantation was clearly supported by English labor. Millions of whites in England rarely or never
saw a black man, but played an active and profitable role
in the manufacture of the articles used to help enslave
that man they did not know.

At the time when forced importation of Negroes to
America began, such racist terms as superior and inferior
were either not much used nor used at all. As we have
seen, the original Portuguese invaders clearly understood
that they were capturing human beings, descendants of
Adam, as they were called. Not yet had there developed
that rationale which would later submerge the African as
a lesser human species. Racial rationalisation did not
easily develop. It took centuries for such attitudes to permeate and saturate white consciousness, and inversely to
affect black thinking.

The only reasoning involved in the original capture of
the blacks was that these people were accessible, unarmed, their color and their culture different; they were
not considered advanced in terms of European mechanics, in the possession of arms, ships, wealth. Yet they
were thought of as people intelligent enough to perform
the complicated tasks of skilled labor. They were taught
"mechanick arts" at the African Forts before their removal. It was their unarmed state, their language barrier,

their lack of an effective organized resistance that made
them enslaveable. In theory the slave trade was war: and
these "Moors" were captives of war, so they would be
put to work as captives of war had always been put to
work.

Through the centuries of the slave trade, the word race
was rarely if ever used. Not, certainly, in the English
language, and that would be the important one, for Englishmen and English-speaking colonials were the primary enslavers. Shakespeare's Shylock uses the words
tribe, nation, but not race. The Moor in *Othello* calls
himself black and the word slave is several times used,
but not race. The word does not appear in the King
James version of the Bible in any context other than as
running a race. The Bible refers to nations and says:
"God made the world and all things therein; and hath
made of one blood all nations of men for to dwell on all
the face of the earth." The Bible, with all its violence
and its incessant warfare between peoples, does not have
racist references to tribes, groups, provinces, nations,
men.

The authoritative *Documents Illustrative of the Slave
Trade,* a compilation of information covering four centuries, contains hundreds of letters, reports, contracts,
trader narratives, bills of lading, Government publications from the year 1441 through 1807 but the references to people is never by, or as, race, only to slaves,
men, youths, captives, a black Mooress, "a stock" of Negroes, poor wretches, specimens, choice slaves, New Negroes, Gold Coast Negroes, likely young boys and girls,
field slaves, negroes, negros, Negroes, Negers, African
Slaves, Property, Natives, sixty head, Whites, Cargo, and
many other similar terms. Whites are not called the white
race; blacks are not called the black race.

As late as 1807, in the last entry in the *Documents,*

which concerns the Act to Prohibit the Importation of Slaves into the United States, there is still no reference to race, but only to slaves, mulattos, persons of colour, African Negroes, West India Negroes, new Negroes, Windward Coast Negro Men, Cargoe of 204 Slaves, Seventy human Beings, Nine Slaves, Nine free Persons, one Girl slave, Persons intended to be sold, Slaves or Persons, Subjects or Inhabitants of Africa, Natives of Africa, Prize of War, Men, Women and Children, Slaves or pretended Slaves—but no reference to race.

As the war into Africa deepened, pigmentation came into use by some slavetraders as a means of establishing separation and control, such as in the case of Captain Snelgrave who had a black man executed because he killed a white.

Even in the cruelties of original capture in Africa, in life at the Forts and the brutalities of the trans-ocean passage, the enslavement was not viewed as an act of racial superiority. In fact the traders, masters and crews had great respect for the slave's ability to resist, his capacity to learn, his resourcefulness in planning revolt. They understood that they were capturing fellow humans.

Still unformed was that element of alienation and brutality which would mature later, in the hard future of a burgeoning concept of Caucasian and Negroid and a rationalisation of "race superiority." Color, though it was a factor from the outset, was centuries away from developing into the evolved negation called "race." That was a superstructure built steadily after the Africans arrived.

A whole panoply of organization was to generate in America's colonial era, and the period of the nation's founding, to provide a continuance of the slave labor system once it was established. Thousands of acts of political "creativity" would enter into the building of a na-

tional pattern that would allow two utterly contradictory concepts—American liberty and American slavery
—to flourish side by side in the American soul.

Tobacco and rice had to be cultivated in the Colonies;
the question was who would do it best and for how little.
In the first thirty or forty years of the various settlements
along the East Coast, so-called indentured servants,
mostly white, were employed on plantations. Even the
earliest Negro help often held this kind of servant status:
they were not owned for life. But within a generation or
so the colonial needs, the market in England for tobacco
and rice, and other economic growth meant that the
plantation operators wanted outright and lifetime slavery
for the African import. By the 1650s the word slave was
in wide daily usage and in various law books of Virginia.
From the time when the slave became as rooted as the
cultivation of tobacco, the legislators entered upon the
greater game of legalising slavery as a national institution. By 1700, it was legally established all the way from
New England down through the Carolinas.

In 1645 Emanuel Downing, father of the later well-
known Sir George Downing, wrote a letter to his brother-
in-law, John Winthrop. This letter, written in London to
John in the Colonies, contained a clearcut vision of a
peopled American Continent, provided blacks could be
obtained to do the hard labor.

He wrote that if upon a just war with the Narragan-
setts the Lord should deliver the red men into their
hands, they might easily get enough men, women and
children to exchange them for African slaves. This, he
wrote, would be more gainful pillage for settlers than
anyone could conceive, for twenty Africans could be
maintained cheaper than one English servant. The En-

glish servants would want freedom to plant for themselves and they wouldn't stay with anyone except for very great wages, whereas slaves aplenty could be bought with a shipload of cheap and available salt. "I do not see," he wrote, "how we can thrive until we get a stock of slaves sufficient to do all our business, for our children's children will otherwise hardly see this great Continent filled with people."

All of this was simple economic talk, with no terminology of superior and inferior peoples, no mention of organic separation of colors; nothing but income, well-being, and someone "to do all our business."

Staying for a moment with the important Downing-Winthrop family, there is the letter George Downing wrote in 1645 to his cousin John Winthrop, Jr. suggesting how John could get a start in the new world. Downing at the age of twenty-two went to the West Indies as a ship's chaplain. He advised John back in England that if he went to Barbadoes he would see a flourishing island. They had bought here that year a thousand Negroes and the more they bought the better able they were to buy, for, he said, in a year and a half, they would earn, with God's blessing, as much as they cost. George advised his cousin that if he could get out of England and take with him some servants to help him on a plantation he could within a very few years procure Negroes ("the life of this place," he put it), out of the increase of the plantation.

English labor itself was thus viewed as a stepping stone to buying slave labor in the Colonies. It is clear that the original permeating motive was the ancient one of procuring labor for nothing.

From 1650 through 1700 importation of slaves from the West Indies to the American mainland received much impetus. In this period the British Crown consolidated heavily along the East Coast. Importations of blacks became so large that English settlers feared they might be outnumbered by the black presence. As that fear set in, the colonists and the mother country sedulously guarded against any such contingency. The peril was alleviated by a continuous free white migration from England into American plantation areas.

The economic voice has always spoken the loudest—then as now. The trader-merchant-financier who paid and supported the theologians and office-holders in the colonies and in England called the tune. One of them, the prosperous Boston merchant, John Saffin, had lived in Virginia between 1654 and 1658, and had there bought and sold slaves. After he became prosperous he moved to Boston where he became a deputy to the General Court and Speaker of the Colonial House of Representatives.

He saw that in Boston, in every house no matter how small, there were one or two Negroes in its service; some houses employed five or six; the slave look of Boston at that time was little different from Virginia. But in the Boston of Saffin's day, the outskirts of the city remained a wilderness. There was no place that a black could escape to, for he would be returned and he must live out his life in service. Saffin regarded this as an eternal verity, an immutably ordained fact of life. With his business ledgers open before him on one side, the Bible on the same table to rationalise his commerce and his control over humans, he and other powerful men like him set the pattern for a commercial New England based on slave and small wage labor. Saffin and other merchants financed slaveships to Africa and ignored the occasional voice of protest against slavery. In the Massachusetts House of Representatives one day, he rose to say that the idea of equal rights was alien to divine sanction.

"There are some to be high and honorable," he said,

"some to be low and despicable, some to be Monarchs, Kings, Princes, and Governors, Masters and Commanders, others to be subjects and to be commanded, servants of sundry sorts and degrees bound to obey; yea, some to be slaves and so to remain during their lives as hath been proved."

The colonies were in constant conflict with the mother country over duties on all imports, especially upon slaves. Disputes with His Majesty about such taxes, which were increasing all through the early 1700s, were to advance the winds of revolution.

In 1761 twenty-five merchants of Philadelphia petitioned the Lieutenant Governor of the Province of Pennsylvania to postpone placing a duty upon the importations of Negroes. They told the official that they had for some time past seen the inconveniences which the inhabitants of Pennsylvania had suffered because of a lack of skilled workingmen and menials. They explained that the reason for this was that many men had enlisted in His Majesty's service and there had been almost a total stop of import of German and other white servants. They didn't want a tax on slaves that would cut down on that import. Slaves would reduce the exorbitant price of white labor, they argued, and in all probability bring the staple commodities back to their usual price. Contending that their purpose was to extend the trade of the province and to act in behalf of the public good, they begged that the duty be postponed.

In petitioning for slaves, not for their own profits but for the common good, as they put it, they helped generate competition between black and white labor.

In South Carolina the situation differed from that in Pennsylvania. There was a serious argument about how many slaves to admit, what controls to set up, or whether to allow slaves at all. Some of the proprietors and poor

whites whose income and livelihood were not dependent
upon slavery took the position that too much importation
of Africans would overrun the region to the detriment of
white labor interested in migrating from Europe. They
argued that the province ought to be congenial to the
settling of Protestants, poor white servants and white
skilled workers.

In April, 1734, the South Carolina Province Council
leaders complained to His Majesty that they were being
overrun with Africans trained to be handicraft tradesmen
to the discouragement of the white subjects of the King.
The English workers had come here to settle and ply
their various occupations but had to give way to people
in slavery, and this, they said, was an obstruction to the
settlement of this frontier with white people.

Two Georgia ministers haggled over these matters in a
correspondence in 1745. The Reverend John Martin
Bolzius, pastor at Ebenezer, Georgia, wrote to the Reverend George Whitefield in a nearby town that white
settlers simply couldn't compete with slave labor: that if
the blacks were not imported, thousands of German
Protestants would be happy to migrate to this region and
they could make the soil yield and make their way. The
other pastor argued that slavery was economically right
for Georgia, and he concluded that he intended to bring
the slaves to the knowledge of Christ.

The Reverend Bolzius doubted that motive and answered Pastor Whitefield: "But, Sir, my Heart wishes
that first the White People in the Colony and Neighbor-
hood may be brought to the Saving and Experimental
Knowledge of Christ." He said that as long as they took
advantage of the poor black slaves, they would increase
the sins of this land to a great height. "And don't believe,
Sir, the language of those persons who wish the introduc-

tion of Negroes under the pretense of promoting their spiritual happiness."

A by-product of the early-day competition of white and black labor was that the defenders of white settlement began a campaign of vituperation against the Negro which has continued across the American centuries. They projected arguments about Negro unreliability; the blacks were dangerous, they stole, they were capable of the rape of white women, they were insurrectionary, they would not fight the Indians, they had no fidelity to His Majesty nor relationship to the English tradition. Ergo: Put a halt to black importation; make the provinces safe for white labor.

What people think and how they feel largely stems from the work relations in which they are engaged. When the same work and employment patterns continued generation after generation so that they involved each man, woman and child in the colonies, of whatever color, a national design was fashioned. Each sale of Negroes at a public auction was an organized example in a different way, and yet the same way, to white and black. Each master act of ordering labor to be performed and each slave act of the performance of that labor was a factor, an activating episode in the development of the separation and alienation of black and white which would permanently characterise the country.

A few of the thousands upon thousands of transactions in the 1700s will illustrate that process. An advertisement in a Beaufort, South Carolina, newspaper in May, 1736, announced the sale of twenty-eight Negroes who had arrived on the mainland three years earlier; it described them as therefore being seasoned or prepared for labor, and they would be sold for ready money or in exchange for a crop on a certain day. This language and activity, multiplied by the thousands, formed master and slave attitudes. "Just imported by John Hawkesworth from Barbadoes a parcel of fine Negroes, Men and Women, and are to be sold at Mrs. Mary Barnsdale's near Mrs. Harris' school." With, of course, impressionable school children available to look at the sale.

Another of the countless advertisements, exchanging and equating humans for commodities reads: "Have sold very well, tho the greatest part on Credit: Extraordinary Encouragement will be given for present Pay and Payment with this Crop: Good Encouragement will be given for ready Pay in Rice, Pitch and Tar."

The merchandising of slaves set the Africans off from the so-called Caucasians; it established the bases for cultures of apartness. "Just Imported, Several very likely Negro Boys and Girls: To be sold by Charles Coffin, at the Seven Stars in Ann Street: as also choice West India Rhum."

But there was also—even then—another side.

Controversy over the merits of slave labor versus free labor raged as incessantly then as talk over civil rights does now—and for about the same reasons. Slave buying all the way from Boston down the East Coast to the Carolinas, going on in almost every city, produced a great doubt in the land. That doubt was often expressed by business leaders. The succinct statements of community heads are often encompassing enough to intimate the very essence of an age or a nation. Fear of what the slave trade would mean to the future of the New World reached a particularly debatable stage in the 1730s. Colonel William Byrd, Jr., of Virginia, in 1736 wrote to England to the Earl of Egmont, who had proposed excluding rum and Negroes from the Colony of Georgia. Byrd approved the exclusion; he told the Earl what slavery was doing to white people: "I wish my Lord we could be blest with the same Prohibition. They import so many Negroes hither, that I fear this Colony will some time or other be confirmed by the name of New Guinea. I am sensible of many bad consequences of multiplying these Ethiopians amongst us. They blow up the pride, and ruin the Industry of our White People, who seeing a Rank of poor Creatures below them, detest work for fear it should make them look like Slaves. Then that poverty which will ever attend upon Idleness, disposes them as much to pilfer as it does the Portuguese, who account it much more like a Gentleman to steal, than to dirty their hands with Labour of any kind."

Colonel Byrd hoped the British Parliament would put an end to it all. He wondered why the Legislature would indulge a few ravenous traders who would freely sell their fathers, their elder brothers, and even the wives of their bosoms, if they could black the faces of their kin and get anything by selling them.

It sometimes seems surprising that a moral cause ever arose and succeeded against the merchant slave-trading class whose power endured for so many centuries. The merchants had a network of relationships that operated in England, in the colonies and in the West Indies. They existed in the thousands over the whole time of the slave trade. Their correspondence flooded the postal systems. Their organization carried great weight in the courts, the general assemblies, all the councils. Their petitions carried the most weight with colonial rulers and with the powers in England. With the shipowners and the plantation owners, they formed the interlocking directorates of the time, determining the mores, the community attitudes. Through their correspondence with one another and with the captains of their ships, with all the buyers and sellers of men, through their discussions of the economy of the day and their lawmaking efforts, their entire network of policy conduct overrode virtually all other influences.

Introduction of slavery to the American continent received official sanction from the Puritan Church, in what was actually an alliance of theology and commerce. The great rationale of the slave trade was that it would civilise a savage people who didn't know, as the English did, who God was.

It is not a pretty picture to conceive of the Puritan divines, men like Increase and Cotton Mather, seated in their colonial studies, poring over the Bible, looking for quotations which would help them rationalise the deeds of the leaders, the merchants, the plantation owners. The Bible is a repository of many contradictions. On one page you find an eye for an eye, on another the Golden Rule. The Mathers culled the Bible for the rights of slavemasters and they found numerous lines, notions, passages, situations, which they applied to the colonial scene. The laity picked this up, repeated it to one another, told themselves that black enserfment was God-ordained, sanctioned by Holy Writ.

They were fond of quoting St. Paul's line that the servant should be returned to his master. Mostly they relied on a passage in Genesis, the curse of Ham, purporting to mean that he who was black was forever branded as outside the pale of humanity.

Early New England theology supported plantation owners and merchants in their problems with white labor that wanted to leave plantations, Indians who would rather die than work with the white man, and Africans who were always trying to break through their strictures. Early American theologians tried to teach those who toiled to be satisfied with their servant and slave lot. Increase Mather, a founding Puritan divine, very early cautioned English indentured servants about disobedience. "You that are servants," he thundered at them from his pulpit, "have you been guilty of stubborn disobedient carriage toward your masters, though God in His word tells you that you ought to be obedient to them with fear and trembling?"

When Cotton Mather took over his father's pulpit he was so irritated by the complete uselessness of the red man as a laborer that he couldn't conceive of the resisting Indians as being human. "We know not when or how these Indians first became inhabitants of the mighty continent, yet we may guess that the Devil decoyed these miserable savages hither, in hope that the gospel of the Lord Jesus Christ would never come to destroy or disturb his absolute empire over them." He beheld in the kidnaped African the best hope for cheap labor and organized some Rules for the Society of Negroes in 1693, one of which was that Negroes disobedient and unfaithful to their masters must be rebuked, denied attendance at church meetings, and runaways must be brought back to their masters and punished. In this, he said, the church was committed to implement St. Paul who had said that servants should be returned to their masters. When some members of his church bought a Negro slave for him, he declared that a "mighty smile of heaven descended upon him."

Even before black slaves were available the clergy wanted its share of Indian slaves. After the Pequot War a minister wrote to Governor Winthrop saying he had heard of a division of women and children in the bay and he put in for his share "viz: a young woman or girle and boy if you thinke good." Reverend Samuel Gray, in the records of Virginia, recovered a runaway slave and had another slave beat the runaway to death. John Bacon, a Puritan of Barnstable, willed that if his slave Dinah survived his wife, Dinah should be sold and the money therefrom should be used in the purchase of Bibles for his heirs.

With the ministers, the merchants and the other leaders of the colonial community working at slavery in that zealous manner, what was there to inspire the illiterate community of white farmers, servants, unskilled workmen, imported convicts, from thinking any better than their leaders taught them to think?

In the *Institutional History of Virginia,* out of a list of about fifteen thousand men and women who signed deeds and depositions, about eight thousand could sign their names but seven thousand could not. There was the fertile soil for absorbing the theological myths: the good earth of New England was a soil of opportunism, illiteracy, and a place for the seeding of strange thought. One does not put down the achievements of the early settlers in their organization accomplishments, the physical feat of settling into a hostile environment, in conquering wilderness, breaking ground for the growing country's later power, glories, triumphs. But the bad seeds of human oppression and human segregation were also sown in that day by those same heroic pioneers.

A certain spirit of the English temper seemed destined to fall absolutely upon the black and only upon the black. It was in the nature of Engand itself during the seventeenth century. Hierarchy ruled within England, whether under Cromwell or the Crown. Status and rank, a conviction of the existence of uppers and lowers, ruled the English mind and polity. There were those who were superior and those who were inferior and this seemed written into the English fabric. During most of those years, including the long Parliament, the Crown was real, powerful, absolute; it dispensed titles, offices, commissions, charters.

Somebody had to be at the bottom of such a scale. Until black slaves were imported into the colonies the ones at the bottom were the indentured white servants who signed a written agreement to go into service for a period of years.

There was a tendency among some colonists to look up to some and to have others whom they could look down upon in the status standings. It was a natural extension for the English mind, for the English lower classes, the workmen, servants, storekeepers, thieves. With black slavery, a true bottom man was found—one who could be imported in quantity and always be recognizable by his skin color. Once this was recognized and accepted among all who were white, the fate of the African on these shores was sealed.

John Rolfe, who married Pocahontas and recorded the history of the first Virginia settlement, complained that the people in his company didn't want to work. They "would all be Keisers, none inferior to the others," he recorded. That implied what was most needed: workers who wouldn't want to be aristocrats, superiors, rulers, "Keisers." When, in 1622, the colonists engaged in a fierce war against the Indians, they were urged to wage it without mercy, with the exception that they should preserve younger Indians "whose bodies may by labor and service become profitable."

All of this ferment was to take concrete philosophic form and expression in the ideas of the leading philosopher of that age of liberal Enlightenment, John Locke.

Locke, born in 1632, was a boy of ten when the colonists were having a war with the Indians. He received a medical education. When he was in his thirties he was already known as a serious thinker. He wrote about theology, finance, government, education and science. He advanced the theory of natural rights, projecting what was called the common sense view. In an age of Papal authority he advocated tolerance of Protestant sects. He theorized on the problems of knowledge, how knowledge could be secured, and what was knowledge and what was untruth. He was convinced that ownership of property was at the root of much of human rights, and that property itself was a power in human rights and in the way communities should be organized. His natural rights ideas were later embodied in the Declaration of Independence. Still later some of his views were incorporated by socialists. Finally his ideas influenced the science of behaviorism and his impact on the role of environment in human relations continues to the present. From about 1700 to 1800 he was the major philosophic influence in the New World. In public life, around the 1650s, he was associated with Crown favorites.

There was the usual blind spot in his thinking, the one which has characterised all of American life since its inceptions. Liberal though he was, advocate of broad, democratic feeling, he shared the careless utilitarian approach to Africans which was characteristic of that age, of the merchants, the slavetraders and the proprietor colonists.

He was the father—in philosophy—of that theory of exclusionism which was to rule American life. This viewpoint held that democracy was for whites, slavery for blacks. Natural rights did not apply to Afro-Americans. In philosophic language Locke spelled out an exclusionist position on the Negro that would ultimately permeate every institution and structure. It took Locke's liberalism itself, the Enlightenment, to evolve a special treatment for the imported black. Through Locke, as through many other influences, of course, primarily commerce and theology, the absolutism of the Crown and the Lords settled like a branding iron on the Negro. He was a kind of sub-man from a convenient black Mars, made by God, to be a servant for life. And one of the more important pre-conditioners of race-thinking, in the early American mind, was Locke's principle of philosophic exclusionism, which spread like a tide across the colonies.

Locke's ideas could be used by various classes. He could be useful to the Crown, also to the colonies. In one of his main philosophic writings he said that slavery was a natural right for some too. Since then apologists for Locke, who credit him with exerting a generally liberal influence upon the developments here during the pre-Revolutionary War time, tend to belittle his beliefs about slavery.

Locke, at the age of thirty-five, provided a group of eight Lords Proprietors with a *Fundamental Constitutions* which would determine how life would be lived in a large tract of New World coastal land once known as the old Virginia domains, but latterly renamed Carolina. He designed a feudal, perhaps a utopian system. He visualised a colonial plantation of aristocrats, with a hierarchy of administrators and servants all the way down the line, with African slaves at the bottom.

The *Fundamental Constitutions* were not to be opposed by anyone. Locke was final: "Since multiplicity of comments serve only to obscure and perplex; all manner of comments and expositions on any part of these Fundamental Constitutions, or any part of the common or statute law of Carolina, are absolutely prohibited."

His idea was that the power and the dominion of the tract or plantation was to be based upon property; that the land was to be so distributed as to work out, first of all, in the interests of the Lords Proprietors. It should function with equality as between the proprietors, but it should all be most agreeable to the monarchy back in England. The main thought was to avoid "erecting a numerous democracy." Nobles and gentry would rule, the social classes would be hereditary: and all this would go on for centuries.

Finally, for anybody who was white in this fine little utopian world, "every freeman of Carolina shall have absolute power and authority over his Negro slaves." It didn't matter whether the slaves were Christians or not; white men, whom he called freemen, were superior.

Locke's theory of how this New World could operate was premised so clearly and exclusively upon slave labor that every inducement was to be made to whites to own human property as well as land.

The *Fundamental Constitutions* provided grants of land in proportion to the number of Negroes a freeman could import into the Colony. Wrote the philosopher:

> For the owner of every negro man or slave brought thither within the first year, 20 acres, and for every woman negro or slave, 10 acres; and all men negroes or slaves after that time and within the first five years, 10 acres; and for every woman negro or slave, 5 acres.
>
> Every Free-man and Free-woman that transport themselves and Servants by the twenty-fifth of March next, being 1667 shall have . . . for every Woman-Servant and Slave 50 acres, paying at most ½ *d* per acre, per annum, in lieu of all demands, to the Lords Proprietors.

From that time on Negroes were brought into Carolina regularly. By 1700 there was a direct commerce between Africa and Carolina. During the period from the first settling of the Carolina region through the time when trade between that place and Africa became direct, rigid codes were established segregating white from black.

Locke's feudal domain never came to pass, but plantation slavery, black importation and the new-born concept of segregation began to spread.

Locke's relationship to the Carolina colony was only an incident in his American influence. His natural rights theory, enunciated many years later, was to spread through the thinking of all. Generally his philosophy enunciated an individualism based upon property which has ever characterised the American scene. But black exclusionism inhered in that outlook also.

So slavery received the philosopher's sanction. It was a stamp of approval from on high; it was theoretical support from a mind, a force, an impellant. Its effect upon merchants, traders, slavers could hardly be exaggerated. This man Locke, whose eyes were on the stars, had made this pronouncement out of his liberal depth of wisdom: "Enslave the African."

It was a source of comfort to the slave merchants, white farmers, plantation owners through that century and the next. They took heart that the brightest intellectual light of England was with them, that he pioneered in blessing and encouraging the slave trade.

Philosophers, theologians, intellectuals, educated proprietors and English gentlemen moved in behind the merchant slavers to give an attitude-making sanction to notions exalting power for the white, exclusion and codes of limitation for the black. They placed an imprimatur of approval upon the policy of separation and enslavement.

The times seemed to need philosophic rationalisation behind the use of slaves, and Locke was there.

The period from about 1640 through 1700 was very formative in the making of America's present-day racially schizophrenic culture. It was a cradle and a crucible for the performance of slavetrading merchants, for the circus trapeze techniques of the philosophers and economic theorists, of theologians.

Most of the discussions of right and wrong still led around to the rationalisation that the use of someone else to do the hard labor at no pay was right and just, God-ordained and good practical economics.

The ex-Britisher on this new American soil tended to drift into a commonalty of his own color and culture. Given a natural hesitancy among people to communicate, colonial organization, deliberately or not, worked from earliest days to keep the three color groups apart. Every agency in the community labored upon these differences, so that by the 1660s a system of laws separating white from both Indian and ex-African began to be built. Whiteness and English tradition were coded into the ownership of American land and into an exclusive and separate civil and human right.

For the colonials, Europe was chiefly England, plus whatever England had derived from the Continent. Attachment in a blood-kin way to the mother country was deep in the early settlers; they had no other awareness of home and country but England. England was family. The relationship to the Old World manifested itself in the American wilderness in countless ways. It would never vanish altogether. It has not vanished yet.

The English set about transplanting the culture of England, even to naming American hamlets and villages after those abroad, with the specific purpose, so one record has it, "as evidence of our unity and likeness to many parts of our native country."

The name Elizabeth City, in Virginia, was changed from the Indian name Koccowtan by appeal to the House of Burgesses. The appeal was made "to change the savage name." And the word "savage," once introduced, was to stay forever to describe the red man. Even in that initiating detail there is Anglo-Saxon tribal persevering, that which would ultimately build to become hegemonic white sway over all.

There was among the colonists a tendency to be sentimental, to take pride in what had gone before, to "remember the blood." The transfer of other English culture, the law, Shakespeare, the Bible, the memory of the Crown—all of this entered the log houses and the timber-built churches. For a long time a tie of iron and blood with the mother country bound them: and all this was to have subtle repercussions upon nonwhites, the red and the black.

Consider how the entire United States is culturally planted with English, Latin and Greek names, signifying our prior cultural tradition in the European West. Consider the almost complete absence of town-city-state-river-mountain names based upon either Africa or the Negro presence in America. This fed the colonist over and over with daily reminders of his own grand past as he conceived it, while enabling him to be ignorant of millenia of African origins. Simultaneously, the colonists told themselves that there was no African history or culture or past—that there was nothing there but a heathen Dark Continent.

On the soil of the United States there are hundreds of thousands of American towns and villages and cities bearing names deriving from England, Holland, France, Germany, and the rest of the European countries; but beyond these, the names go back two thousand years to the Senecas, Ovids, Ciceros of the Greeks, and the

Romes, Venices and Florences of early Italy. Multiply these revered symbols with an overlay of old English names, York, Boston, Washington: and finally, when you do get a non-European name, it is an American Indian name like Cayuga or Onondaga.

But the Negro looks around and he sees no Tanganyikas and no Masai or Mandingo landmarks on American soil. His continent and past have been excluded and he has been made to feel he had none of any consequence. He stares out and around and beyond through the maze of Anglo-European stamps, labels, records, names, and finally he can actually find a Cairo (population 12,000) along the Mississippi. If he looks through American history he will find that he was making a symbolic beginning at the time of the Gold Rush to California in 1849: out there they have a Nigger Hill.

Philip Freneau, the Revolutionary War poet, saw the power of the relationship between the new American tradition and the mother country. He labored in a poignant envy of the power of the English poets, the beauty of the English language. The tremendous force of the King James version of the Bible, its poetry and cadence, challenged him, and in his propaganda verses he could never equal the strength, the imagery and sibilance of the mother tongue's great poets. But he was a picture of the American cousin a hundred and fifty years after the first colonization as he and the others of his time drank from the teats of England. Wrote this Poet Freneau:

London, Britannia's pride, that powerful isle,
The land of heroes, that prolific soil,
Where half its harvests from its filth have sprung,
And half its soil is formed of men they hung;
—London, whose commerce through the world extends,
London, the ship-loads of her novels sends,

London, sweet town, where scribbling is a trade,
From the vain Countess to her chamber-maid;
London, a tyrant in the times by-past
Will fix our manners and our fate at last.

The more we drew upon the European and Western heritage, introducing into our midst English language and law, European folkways, music and art. Greek tradition and philosophy, Latin teaching and history, and Judaic-Christian moral and religious values, the more we crowded out, blanketed over and wiped out the human and historical value which the continent-owning black man of antiquity and pre-European conquest possessed. The more we borrowed from the Old World, transplanting its science, industry and mechanical craft, the more we blotted out the African memory, the African world.

Slavetraders themselves were unquestionably the originators of the sex-race-color complex which was fated to bedevil the conscience and codes of the American nation. The traders were promiscuous with their female purchases and set patterns for the use of African women which were followed by crews on the slaveships headed for the West Indies. Since one of the purposes of the capture of women was to provide breeders for the New World whose offspring would work the plantations or take care of the houses, many a mulatto infant conceived at sea or along the Gold Coast was born in the West Indies a few months after the voyage across the Atlantic. These offspring were sold into slavery.

Within three years after the arrival of the first twenty Africans, the Virginia colonial legislature fashioned a law establishing a fine for coition between white and Negro servants. But the practice of black and white sexual association had begun and it would never halt.

Hugh Davis, a white man, was the first known male victim of cohabitation with a black woman. Virginia documents record that he was whipped for "defiling his body in lying with a negro."

Historians have lingered over this single case, one that stands in some isolation for some years from other recorded acts of the separation of black and white sexually. Thomas Wertenbaker in his book *The First Americans* said that there were a few cases on record of white women servants being found guilty of intimacy with Negro slaves. "Having just arrived from England, they had not yet acquired the feeling of racial antipathy for the African." Interestingly stated, for it suggests how the colonial leaders had to work at inculcation of attitudes. Another historian, Curtis P. Nettles in *The Roots of American Civilization* suggests that there was a general crossing of black and white and male and female which "gave a problem" to the colonial legislatures.

Throughout the actual acts of the lawmakers there runs the poignant theme of how people coming together for the first time without prejudice, without animosities, were prepared to live together, until a rule of force bent itself to the task of inventing a separate order of mankind.

The significance of this early-day attraction between white and black is simply that the gulf of the sexual taboo was not there by nature nor by the desire of the settling people. It developed with the policy makers.

It would become fashionable generations later to ascribe bitterness, bias and violence primarily to the poor whites. Whatever the merits of these assertions for a later time, in the early period the decrees on segregation of the sexes, as all other laws of bias, came from the legislating, ruling figures and families.

The question of sexual relations between black and white bothered the lawmakers and plantation operators morally and economically. The entire future of cheap labor in America hung on this touchy question of sex. If there were free relationships between black and white, if there were mixed issues of that social combination, if there were not one segment of labor available to pit against another, how would the economy advance? As George Downing put it, twenty Moors could be had for the cost of one white servant, and if that situation changed how could the New World be built, how could business prosper?

Keeping white and black apart sexually presented itself to the colonial founders as a ready-made, obvious and hopefully easy way to control the situation. What they would not foresee was that this policy, continuing for generations and centuries through wars and revolutions, would result in a complex and neurotic social organization. While it is customary to ascribe the country as being founded on principles of freedom of religious worship, conscience, free enterprise, other nobilities, and while much of that is true, in practice the economy of the nation had its inceptions with a more enduring, more rigid principle—sexual separation of the colors for purposes of acquisition of land, wealth and power.

In Virginia, the classic state for development of white-nonwhite relationships, there was from earliest colonial legislatures up through recent years a persevering effort to legislate interracial sexual relations out of existence. Year after year for centuries the legislature of that State renewed its drive to keep the colors apart, threatening jail, death, whipping for black or white of either sex who crossed the line. Proof of the fact that this was much ignored was in the reiteration of the law annually.

In the early period, before codes and customs were clearly worked out, liaison between black and white servants was frequent and not always clandestine. In the Carolina country, mulatto population around 1750 was noticeable in communities everywhere. So much so that this led to a debate about how to halt black immigration, or how to increase migration of Europeans. The Reverend John Martin Bolzius worried about the further admission of Africans to his part of the country and wrote to another pastor: "I am sure that if the Trustees allowed to one thousand White settlers so many Negroes, in a few years you would meet in the streets, as in Carolina, with many Malattoes and many Negro children, which in process of time will fill the colony."

Mostly the mulatto population has been attributed to white male rule over the black woman. At a later time, after 1800, when slavery became fiercest in the South, Negro women were reduced to a maximum subordination where resistance to white male overture could result in beating, burning or lynching.

With time, and the full maturation of the race concept, a whole complex of special psychological attitudes developed, with white man, white woman, black man and black woman each occupying a different relationship one to the other. Special beliefs, myths, fantasies and problems have become associated with each. Relationships peculiar to this blocked but interlocked foursome were to develop, and these distended and warped psychological attitudes, which will be discussed later, are now in national currency.

In the early days English slavetraders, dealing with the New England Colonies and with West Indies planters, were much concerned about the planters' capacity to pay their debts. The Company of Royal Adventurers Trading into Africa, in a petition to the King, complained that they had given the planters a long time for payment so as to encourage them. They were now forty thousand pounds sterling in debt to the petitioners who found themselves very much abused by the intolerable delays of payment.

Later, as slavery spread, the English adopted a different attitude. They decided that the way to control the colonials was to have them in their debt. So long as the New World was retained as an agrarian and dependent region, remaining one continuous, large-scale plantation, control could be maintained. With the merchants, planters and slavedealers answerable in court for their debts, England would be dominant, the slave trade could continue indefinitely; Liverpool and London would go on prospering.

The planters came to live in fear of the British. Communications between colonial merchants during the years before the Revolution were so filled with the burden of debt to London and Liverpool that, as one planter wrote, the Guinea Factors would not deal with colonial slavers but only with selected English dealers.

Arthur Middleton, one of the richest slave-owners in South Carolina, wrote in 1727 to Governor Francis Nicholson that the planters were uneasy in their private circumstances, for the great number of Negroes that had been imported within three or four years had run them prodigiously in debt, and their creditors pursuing them had put them in desperate circumstances.

The planters' "desperate circumstances" was passed on to the slaves. Feeling themselves the victims of the British, so much in their control that they regarded themselves as "a species of British-owned property," the planters turned the more mercilessly against the field hands, the demand for wider cultivation of crops intensifying.

The British, remote from plantation operation, were in

the position of being distant but actual screw-turners, forcing the plantation owner to secure more productivity from his slaves. This double weight, English and domestic, pressed the black to the soil ever more severely.

In the period between 1700 and the outbreak of the Revolutionary War the English did everything in their power to intensify the slave trade and to make the colonies a totally slave-operated world. Among the colonists there was diverse opinion. In some places slavery ceased to be profitable and planters wished to give up the institution. Some moral voices were being raised against slavery. But another large and decisive segment of the planters, indebted to the English but caught up in the only business they knew and believing they would get out of debt and eventually prosper, fought for the retention of chattel slavery.

While this domestic quarrel was afoot the power of the mother country over the colonies intensified and finally, after about 1750, became totally oppressive.

Most of the processes in the making of the sovereign white mind were by now quite fully formed. But another nodal point was at hand: The Revolutionary War and the compromise Constitution which followed.

Just as surely as Betsy Ross sewed that flag, the events of 1776-1785 were to sew into the national mentality a wavering quality: an ambivalence called conscience. This conscience would turn out to be useless to Negroes, but convenient to whites because it made many think they were doing something about the civil rights of slaves and free Negroes. Conscience enabled them to confuse thinking with action.

America's split personality, its white sovereignty and

its black exceptionalism, sprang alive in this, the Revolutionary period.

The Declaration of Independence, with its credo that all men are created equal, was launched in a spirit of white inclusion and the practice of black exclusion. The slaveholders pressured Thomas Jefferson into removing from the Declaration an antislavery passage which accused the King of England of keeping open a market "where men should be bought and sold."

But many New Englanders and Southerners were not yet ready to regard the ex-Africans as men. The persistent policy struggle between the pro-slavery and antislavery people was often won by pro-slavery advocates. Although, before the Revolution and after it, humane voices pointed out the contradiction between a war for liberation which tolerated a shameless slavery at home, pro-slavery voices were to prevail.

The ambivalence, the conscience theme, is organic to our history and is best illustrated in the interior life of the man we know today as the father of our country.

No one will gainsay the greatness of Washington, his patriotic valor, his military excellence, his fortitude. But to the end, to his death, he retained a lifetime character of practical exceptionalism toward the slave.

He was a fourth-generation slaveholder; he was trained by his father to work slaves, and his precision work as a surveyor apparently helped refine him in the tasks of securing efficiency and a profit from his plantation. As a young man inheriting an estate and slaves upon the death of his father, he went about his plantation measuring the amount of lumber his slaves could cut in a certain time and thereafter establishing for them the amounts they should cut. He could warn a boy slave to get to work properly and rebuke the father of the boy. He bought and sold slaves, advertised for runaways, sold one runaway to the West Indies in exchange for which he hoped to get molasses, rum, a barrel of limes, a pot of tamarinds and ten pounds of candy.

In 1771, when he was being taxed for the ownership of eighty-seven slaves, he hired a carpenter, Benjamin Buckler, to work for about ten months training four Negroes in the trade of carpentry. The agreement called upon Buckler to "oblige himself to use his utmost endeavors to hurry and drive them on to the performance of so much work as they ought to render."

That is not to say that he was necessarily a harder slavemaster than others; the evidence is that he was more humane. References to Negroes in his diaries reveal numerous acts of consideration as well as stern requirements. He let his Negroes go fishing occasionally and he urged his overseers to treat sick Negroes with humanity and tenderness. At the same time he restricted slaves to the plantation when they were well and forbade them to mix with "strange Negroes."

By 1770 Washington had already been brought into the orbit of organized opposition to King George. Only eleven days after he purchased two Negroes, on June 11th, 1770, he signed the resolutions of the Association for the Counteraction of Various Acts of Oppression on the Part of Great Britain. This was a resolve of American colonist-slaveholders not to import any more slaves after the following November 1st.

Washington agreed to that, not because he was ready to relinquish slavery, but because he, like other colonists, was vexed with the mother country for a long series of acts of economic oppression and he was specifically ired with English slave merchants.

Yet in 1772 Washington bought five more slaves. He

was, in fact, still deeply involved with slave-buying almost to the eve of the outbreak of the Revolutionary War.

A few months after his purchase of the five slaves he was elected Chairman of a Fairfax County delegation to the Virginia State Convention. Slaves had become a burden to the State of Virginia by now; they were a threat to white rule, and more numerous than needed for the cultivation of the plantations. One Fairfax County resolve declared that it was "our most earnest wishes to see an entire stop forever put to such a wicked, cruel and unnatural trade."

But when Washington was named Commander in Chief of the Continental forces he still had the psychology of a slaveholder. Troubles with the mother country were one thing, troubles with slaves were another.

The evidence is that he would rather have waged the war against Britain without the aid of Negroes, free or slave. On October 8th, 1775, a Council of War was held in Boston, General Washington convening with other generals, and there was unanimous agreement to reject slaves and free Negroes from the Continental Army. In fact, in spite of the awareness by all the Revolutionists that the Negro himself had the right to be in revolt, the High Command directed guards to "seize and confine till sunrise any Negro found straggling about any of the roads and villages near the encampments at Roxbury or Cambridge."

By November His Majesty's Crown were trying to recruit Negroes to the British cause; as a result, a few weeks later, Washington was forced to instruct recruiting officers to give serious consideration to free Negroes desirous of enlisting in the American cause. He decided to allow their enlistment unless the Continental Congress disapproved of it. To take that step Washington had to oppose his generals and renounce the policy of exceptionalism which the colonial military men in general approved.

All of this illustrates how, in the mind of a slaveholder, albeit a strong and great man, the hard facts of life alone forced Washington to retreat from his inner conviction that Negroes should not be allowed to fight on the side of freedom: the crisis, the peril, the absolute need in terms of survival determined his change of plan. Not moral conviction. Nor concern.

Eighty-seven slaves of his own could change none of Washington's thinking, not his prejudices, emotions, feelings of ownership and supremacy. But a half million Negroes who might, from irk, resentment and centuries of pain and provocation, switch over to the enemy—that was a group of a different size.

During the next two years both free Negroes and slaves were employed in the Continental Army. In 1778, there were more than fifty Negroes in each of seven brigades of Washington's Army. Once, earlier, the General, as slaveholder, had done everything he could to keep such men from asserting themselves as men, teaching them as little as possible, expecting them to obey the harsh civil codes of Virginia. Now he was handling these same men as soldiers, patriots, Americans, as new men in the making. The ambivalence begins to emerge.

By January of 1778, Washington had no objections at all to the enrollment of a battalion of Negroes from Rhode Island, as a means of that state bringing its full quota into the Continental Army. This is a much different Commander than the one who, several years earlier, had asked, "Ought not Negroes to be excluded from enlistment?" Moreover, by now Washington was not averse to employing as wagoners free Negroes from Carolina, Virginia and Maryland, and using them for supply purposes in the South.

The question of the black man, his courage, patriotism, human worth, continued to gestate in Washington's mind through the remainder of the war. He appeared to sanction the raising of a battalion of three thousand black troops in South Carolina, though he did call it a "moot question." The fact is that in various battles the black troops acquitted themselves heroically, a circumstance which Washington noticed, especially at Point Bridge, New York, and at the Battle of Monmouth.

By the end of the war the question of the Negro slave, the Negro soldier and the dawning Negro American was a massive one. How would the newly-forming nation handle the black? Had his participation in the war won for him place and vindication, citizenship and freedom?

General Lafayette knew that Washington was thinking along these lines. On February 5th, 1783, he wrote a letter to Washington in which he suggested: "Now, my dear General, that you are going to enjoy some ease and quiet, permit me to propose a plan to you, which might become greatly beneficial to the black part of mankind. Let us unite in purchasing a small estate, where we may try the experiment to free the Negroes, and use them only as tenants. Such an example as yours might render it a general practice . . ."

Washington received that letter shortly before peace was announced to the troops. He answered by saying that the plan was a striking evidence of the benevolence of Lafayette's heart. "I shall be happy to join you in so laudable a work; but will defer going into a detail of the business till I have the pleasure of seeing you."

It must have been only a feint, for in the post-Revolutionary War days, Washington, though he had

learned much respect for the blacks, was still acting am-
bivalently as matters of Negro ex-soldiers' rights arose.
With one he wanted a full-scale inquiry when the black's
former slaveholder asked for his return into slavery.
(There had been a time in Washington's thinking when
no Negro had any right that could take him into any kind
of American court.) Yet he was on the hunt for his own
slaves who had gone to New York, because on April
28th, 1783, he wrote to Commissioner Daniel Parker,
empowered to inspect the embarkation of the British:
"Some of my own slaves, and those of Mr. Lund Washington who lives at my house, may probably be in New
York, but I am unable to give you their description—
their names being so easily changed, it will be fruitless to
give you. If by chance, you should come at the knowledge of any of them, I will be much obliged by your
securing them, so that I can obtain them again."

In June, as the Army was demobilized, Washington
sent a letter to the Governors of the States in which he
called for union of the states under one head. He urged
all to "a sacred regard to public justice," and he asked
the peoples of all the colonies to "forget their local prejudices and policies; to make those mutual concessions,
which are requisite to the general prosperity; and in some
instances, to sacrifice their individual advantages to the
interest of the community." If he had in mind in any of
these provisions the position of the blacks, it wasn't specifically mentioned.

Washington resumed post-war life as a Virginian, a
slaveholder and a planter. In August of 1784, Lafayette
returned to America. Apparently the Frenchman was
still of a mind to build that little colony of free Negroes,
conceiving them as tenants. But if he and Washington
discussed the matter again, there is no record of it.

Yet Lafayette had strong feelings about freeing blacks

and went ahead with his own experiment in the French Guiana colony of Cayenne. He started the project by himself, giving toward it a hundred thousand francs. Washington heard of this and wrote to the Marquis, congratulating him upon his benevolence. In a letter sent May 19th, 1786, Washington called the project "a generous and noble proof of your humanity. Would to God," he went on, "a like spirit might diffuse itself generally into the minds of the people of this Country. But I despair of seeing it. Some petitions were presented to the Assembly, at its last session, for the abolition of slavery, but they could scarcely obtain a reading. To set the slaves afloat at once would, I really believe, be productive of much inconvenience and mischief; but by degrees it certainly might, and assuredly ought to be affected and that too by legislative authority."

Washington had gone far from his early upbringing even to express such sentiments. Whatever slavery was, it was no longer right, and he could say so. But he was paralyzed to act.

In letter after letter to American figures he repeated that he would like to see slavery abolished, that he could no longer buy or sell slaves. Yet in November of 1786 he took some slaves in payment of a debt. "Although I have great repugnance to encreasing my slaves by purchase; yet as it seems so inconvenient for you to make payment by other modes, than those you have proposed, and so injurious as not to be accomplished at a less loss than fifty or more pct., I will take five or more negroes of you, if you can spare such as will answer my purpose upon the terms offered in our former letter . . ."

Only a few months before the Constitutional Convention in May of 1787 he asked a man named Henry Lee to buy a slave for him. He couldn't buy it himself as he was principled against increasing his number of slaves by purchase, but would Lee do it for him? Washington did say that if the slave under consideration, a certain brick-layer, had a family from whom he must be parted by this purchase, Washington would decline the purchase.

Locked inside the economic institution of slavery him-self, possessed by his plantation, his whole treasure, still he had seen enough of man's fight for liberty to know that enslavement was wrong. He had crystallized his con-science.

At long last the Constitutional Convention was held, with Washington presiding over it. He was an impartial chairman, allowing the others to debate all issues—including slavery.

The Constitution was formed in compromise over many issues, including the slave issue. On this, the stipu-lation was that the Negro would count as only three-fifths of a person, and the slave trade was to be abolished after 1808. It was Washington's view that unless this com-promise was entered into, there would be no union of the colonies; they would dissolve at this convention and the delegates would go home: there would be thirteen differ-ent nations.

From the instant of the formation of the Union no more crucial question was presented to the newly pro-claimed President Washington than this. The civil rights cauldron was the first to be placed upon the new Ameri-can stove.

Within a year Quakers petitioned the President for abolition of the slave trade and emancipation of the blacks generally. The Quaker petition, debated in the Congress, resulted in a prediction of Civil War to be declared by the South in the event of emancipation.

As the fight over importations of slaves persisted and as Washington presided over these matters like a conscience-stricken judge, he continued the operation of his farms by slave labor at Mount Vernon. His overseers reported to him weekly on the labor performed by his slaves. The President wrote to one of his managers that he didn't like the way his slave Ben was behaving. ". . . if a stop is not put to his rogueries and other villanies, by fair means and shortly, I will ship him off (as I did Waggoner Jack) for the West Indies where he will have no opportunity of playing such pranks as he is at present engaged in."

Still, in 1794, he wanted to get rid of some of his western lands, for he had a thorn in his side now which wouldn't let him rest. "I have another motive which makes me earnestly wish for these things—it is indeed more powerful than all the rest—namely to liberate a certain species of property, which I possess very repugnantly to my own feelings."

A little later in the same year, Washington, who had a vision now about the American nation shaping up, wrote to a friend, Alexander Spotswood, that if he had his way he wouldn't twelve months later be possessed of one slave. Ominously and predictively, he said, "I shall be happily mistaken, if they are not found to be a very troublesome species of property ere many years pass over our heads."

Even later than this President Washington advertised for a runaway slave, although he didn't want his name to appear in any advertisements north of Virginia.

The pendulum within him swung and swung.

In Washington's Farewell Address to the nation he bypassed mention of slavery. He was again motivated by the idea of Union preservation, as he had been motivated in his silence at the Constitutional Convention.

Back at Mount Vernon, presiding over his slaves unhappily, looking off into the American future, Washington wrote to his nephew: "I wish from my soul that the legislature of this State, could see the policy of gradual abolition of slavery. It might prevent much future mischief."

Thus Washington spoke out frequently in private and in letters, but no general public moral statement by him on slavery seems to exist: not as a speech, nor as a Constitutional recommendation.

In the last year of his life he complained to another nephew that the burdens of the plantation were too much for him, that he wouldn't sell his slaves and he couldn't hire them out nor disperse the families. What could he do? he asked. "Something must (happen) or I shall be ruined; for all the money, in addition to what I raise by crops and rents, that have been received for Lands, sold within the last four years to the amount of Fifty thousand dollars, has scarcely been able to keep me afloat."

When he died not long afterward he owned one hundred and twenty-four slaves in his own right, one hundred and fifty-three Dower Negroes, and forty other Negroes on lease. He willed that the slaves he personally owned be freed upon the death of his wife.

In Washington's relationship to his slaves we have in a microcosm the American story: the ambivalence, the moral recognition that slavery is wrong, but an organic inability or a persisting unwillingness to put the ax to the roots.

Americans, trying to understand themselves, have often spoken of the formation of American character or the conscience of Americans, and there has been much theory about when, where and how such character formed. At what point did our national personality, if there is such, take form? Historians, philosophers and other observers have meant by this exclusively white Americans, as if the Negro were never upon our soil.

One such historian, Henry Pratt Fairchild, said that the American mind (white) was a completed task by the time of the Revolutionary War. In his opinion America had by then emerged as a genuine nationality in its own right and he thought of later arrivals as being admitted into a going nationality and not as helping to build one.

Within the English-European unity into which the white colonials organized, there developed a large pool of white commonalty. Colonists deriving from the entire European variety coalesced within a few generations in a breed calling itself American. The Britons were central to this amalgam. Cotton Mather described the English influence as overswaying all else: "Well may New England lay claim to the name it wears and to a room in the tenderest affections of its mother, the Happy Island!"

The Happy Island peoples provided the main coloration and tenor of language and ways to the newly developing American. Intermarriage flourished from earliest times up through the Revolution. Dutch, Swedish, Welsh, Finns, French Huguenots, Germans interwedded and interwelded in this American blending of peoples. Immigrants from these and other European countries brought with them for transplanting here their songs, dances, crafts, language, ideas, myths, religions, superstitions, farm and industrial methods, even dress customs and manners. The old ways gradually underwent modifications on the new continent but the color-cultural identity persisted untouched.

While that was in process, slavery, casting the Afro-American inside a different crucible, ground up all the varying African tribal and continental origins, vestiges, physiognomies, into a new mixture. Here too was a new

American, a new character and a new conscience in formation, but nobody knew what it was, nor much cared to examine it. This personality too was, by the time of the Revolution, on the way to becoming a new type or figure. There was by now a "white American" and something like a "Negro American."

The Founding Fathers, when they wrote into the Constitution a continuation of the slave trade until 1808, injected into our national mores the conditions which now go by the name of civil rights violation. Then, early in the 1800s, when the invention of the cotton gin gave a new impetus to chattel slavery, resulting in new irons being placed upon the Afro-American, there was a further widening of that gulf which had already been pretty well built by the time Washington took command of the Army.

The fact is that the Constitution was built for the preservation and protection of white European immigrants who by intermarriage merged into "the first Americans." The Afro-American was so far beneath consideration by the framers of the Constitution that he wasn't even mentioned. The formulators of America's fundamental law were more fearful of the prospect of pressure from lower class whites than from anything else. The moral issue of slavery, though it made an appearance in the Constitutional debates, was at last sublimated and compromised.

James Madison, Father of the Constitution and a two-term President, at the time of the writing of *The Federalist* papers, seeking to work out a compromise with the slaveholders, decided on a policy of subordinating the slave issue. He made a subtle appeal to the Southern planters to come into the Union on grounds that if they were ever threatened by domestic insurrection from the black side, they could have the protection guaranteed by a Federal Union. Madison incidentally used the creeping anatomical-racial term, "species of population." Wrote this early American spokesman: "I take no notice of an unhappy species of population abounding in some of the states who, during the calm of regular government are sunk below the level of men; but who, in the tempestuous scenes of civil violence, may emerge into human character and give a superiority of strength to any party with which they may associate themselves."

Sixteen signers of the Constitution were slaveholders. They may have been concerned for the character and future of themselves and other whites, but no concept existed at the time that considered the black American as part of American character or even as part of the human scene. The Negro was so clearly left outside of our first considerations that an ultimate profound repercussion, as Washington anticipated, was inevitable.

It was the Constitution itself, more than any other document, that sealed the formation of two national-tribal types on the American continent. The consequence was the establishment of a living, built-in schism perennially active, generating constantly two differentiated beings and projecting each into a future that could only be frictional and warlike.

The processes in back of this national schism had developed in stages that took about a hundred and fifty years. First was the incubator process at the Forts in Africa and the Middle Passage. Second the acceleration process in the development of slave status over a period of a few generations. Third was a transformer process—the white conquest and settlement of the territories, with the understanding that whites were not to enslave whites but to reserve the enslaving process exclusively for the man from Africa. A fourth and determining stage, building on the prior developments, was psychological: the remaking of the minds of both white and black.

Gradually the white mind was developing its sovereign character—all whites sovereign over all blacks—and refractively there crystallised a new human type called the Negro slave.

By the time the Constitution was ratified, the whole manufactory was ablaze.

UP TO THE REVOLUTION

It is one of the misfortunes of the advance of science in the modern period that its results, which are actually morally neutral, have been invoked or distorted so as to support one or another political position. It is the saddest of all that the modern race concept has as its origin, in part, one of the really grand schemes of science.

Carolus Linnaeus, in the mid-1700s, as a young botanist enthralled with the exquisite color, form and architecture of nature, conceived the idea of classifying the multiferous forms of life. It was an audacious notion, for anyone who has stopped to consider for even a single moment one square foot of any field will be amazed at the kaleidoscopic diversity of nature. But young Linnaeus had a grand concept; there was a world of perfect forms, archetypes that were immutable and eternal. Each individual form of nature, each example of the various plants and animals, were copies of this archetype. To him the world of nature was not a continuum, but a system of structures out of which definition could be found. We could only know these archetypes by their morphology, and it was upon the basis of morphological type that forms could be grouped, classified and named. Linnaeus proceeded to undertake a description of this nature and he founded taxonomy, a science of description which had as its motivation an almost God-based devotion to the existence of order in nature.

Linnaeus' use of categories such as *species, genus, race,* inspired a long succession of researchists, scientists, observers, to extend Linnaeus' findings and to strike off into other directions. One of the submovements or off-shoots of the taxonomical approach was the development of a so-called science of ethnology, a realm of inquiry which undertook to examine the diversity of the human animal.

It is not a great extrapolation from the world of immutable, God-created archetypes, of which all the forms in this world are somewhat imperfect copies, to the idea of races forever separate and unequal and created by God in all His wisdom to be separate and unequal.

Late in the eighteenth century, from about the time of the American Revolution onward, the *species* and *genus* approach began to be applied to human beings, and the word *species* first began to make its appearance in the writings of American and English statesmen. With this came also the word *race*. And here we begin to find the valuable, innocent, pioneering work of Linnaeus becoming transformed by practical, race-making politics into a huge game, a diversion and distortion, which was to unleash a flood of bigotry all over the Western hemisphere, which was to lead on to world-wide politics of violence against vulnerable "species" and establish patterns of racial absolutes in the United States. It was also to play an important part through its capillaries, veins and arteries of development, in the rise of the other racial myths that would later devastate Europe.

After the Constitution was agreed upon and the slave trade deepened and hardened, as slave importations increased in the Southern Colonies, as the cotton gin gave rise to the need for hundreds of thousands more slave workers in the fields, great need arose to find a means to justify the evolution of the often sentimentalized Negro prison camps called cotton plantations.

An English philosopher like John Locke, a Fundamentalist, had moved into useful and contemporary philosophical speculations from the Biblical premise of the world's origin. But a big breakaway from the Bible was well on its way after Linnaeus. Biologists and others caught glimpses of a very old earth. In the Linnaean tradition, they began classifying everything in nature, including animals. In the latter system of classification man began to make his appearance as a higher animal. It wasn't long before this kind of thinking, construed as a legitimate development of science, spawned the classification of man into those various and assertedly immutable "races" which have currency even now.

After the Revolution and around the time of the organization of the Constitution, the prestige of Linnaeus here, in England, and everywhere in Europe was overwhelming. Thomas Jefferson admired Linnaeus and sought to introduce the science of taxonomy, classification, to the American scene. Terms like *species, genus, race* took on sophisticated meaning; slaveholders and statesmen fell in with a convenient and useful terminology. The slave became known as a "species of property." Washington, Jefferson, Madison began using that formulation. The word "race" to describe the Negro had a conviction that the slave system seized upon. The term, virtually unknown as an application to humans in 1750, was by 1790 in general use. No other expression carried the force, connotation, or conviction of this new word.

Insofar as the Linnaean pioneerings made contributions to legitimate biology, the taxonomist tradition was beneficial, but the branch of it that went into contemporary sociology and politics became a different matter.

In the slave trade itself the traders continued to refer to their captives as Negroes, stock, Africans, slaves, never using the term *race*. But the American statesmen, having done the best they could in completing a constitution of compromise and needing to support their creation, more and more came to use the botanical terminology. *Race* was a tough, unbeatable word. It had

implication that defied argument. It had "scientific" basis.
You could capitalize the word *Race* and it was then no
more debatable than the term God.

On this soil was a unique pool for the development of
"ethnological" doctrine. As Indian, Negro and white remained generally apart, the separation itself invited ex-
aminations for characteristics, classification, speculation.
That is, Indians and blacks fell under examination, not
the white. Typical titles of the time were an *Essay on the
Causes of Variety of Complexion and Figure in the
Human Species,* by Samuel S. Smith, published at Philadelphia in 1787, or Benjamin Barton's *New Views of the
Origins of Tribes and Nations of American Indians,* issued in 1797. But long before those publications, a much
more daring innovator, and one of the most unscientific
of all, Thomas Jefferson himself, plunged into speculations which were to influence the whole school of racial
ethnologists. It is strange, anomalous and an unhappy
matter that he who may have been the most sophisticated
intellectual of his day and a major contributor to the
founding of democratic civilization should have also projected a line of thinking which has been the delight of
informed racists ever since.

Chorales of praise have been uttered to the glories of
President Thomas Jefferson, to his august and benevolent rule, his wisdom, his literary style, his great Declaration of Independence, his official pronouncements, and
to his voluminous letters numbering, so it has been reported, more than fifty thousand. The time of his Presidency, the two terms, was one in which he must stabilize
the ship, after Washington and others had helped launch
it; and Jefferson did it. His general breadth, his interest in
science, the humanities, and national growth became a
model for all statesmen.

But where Washington grew in conscience even though he was incapable of public action or pronouncement in the slave's behalf, Jefferson as he grew older became cold and intellectually reasoning about the slave: the more he thought and wrote of the Afro-American the more he viewed the "species" around him as a kind of graduate ape, dehumanised, unassimilable. Civil rights leaders have either soft-pedaled Jefferson's influence, sought to sublimate it altogether, or tried to drag positive affirmations out of Jefferson's great reputation. Advocates of Negro rights pointed to Jefferson's most famous five words: *"All men are created equal."* And they asked: Does not this apply to us?

Such an approach to the meaning of Jefferson falls far short of what his impact was and where his racial views finally led him. Jefferson is a waystation in the growth and diffusion of racial prejudice in America. He has as great a claim to exclusionism, myopia, diagonalism with regard to the black American as any other Southerner who lived. Because of his vast influence, because he was twice President and because his words have gone on generation after generation ever since, we cannot in all candor here avoid noting his views and contribution to the reservoir of racialism. Jefferson was fluent and ingenious in the projection of the myths of his time.

The slave fascinated him. He beheld on his own plantations and across the land a devitalised human figure, deprived of his native land, denied education, leisure, time to think, without the culture of either continent. Yet Jefferson viewed the black, by now moulded into a work machine, as the finished product of nature, with the full potential realised. On paper, in his letters, in his *Notes from Virginia,* he could acknowledge that the black had been under force, seized, kidnaped ·and conceivably somewhat handicapped therefore, but in the same breath Jefferson fell back into his fixed conception that the Afri-

can was never any more than what he was on the plantations and could never be more. He looked at the often
abject, dehumanised slave who sometimes had a wild un-
comprehending, trapped look in his eye, and Jefferson
asked himself: How could this figure be part of the
human race? And his answer was that this was an animal, a "species," not a human being, not entitled to be
treated as were white men and women.

The closer he looked at the uneducated, limited, impoverished, ill-clothed, guttural-sounding slaves about
him, the more did sympathy—and his understanding—
vanish. Unable to see that he and many generations of
whites like himself had invented this figure, had demol-
ished the African man and substituted in that place a half-
human workmachine, he could only perceive the end result. He did not grasp how much had been deadened,
destroyed. In the colonial generations there had been
blotted out of hundreds of thousands of Africans nearly
all recollection of Africa. Little was left of their original
world but some music, a few art influences that crept into
the product of ironworkers and housebuilders, dancing
habits and rhythms of the old forgotten continent, and
some folk recollections on the level of enduring mother
wit. Seized from hundreds of varying tribes from all over
Western Africa, the Africans possessed great physical
variety, numerous languages, many religious backgrounds. All of that had been ground into nothingness.
What stood before Jefferson was what stood before other
plantation owners—men and women deliberately dehu-
manized into beasts of burden.

Jefferson's thinking on slaves fed his pen in unique
and candid ways. He could write in 1782 when Virginia
had 270,000 slaves and 296,000 free persons, "This blot
on our country increases as fast or faster than whites."

James Madison could conceive that a slave mass

which might one day mount a great resistance could, through this, re-humanize itself. So could Alexander Hamilton. But Jefferson bore a taint of alienation which he could never suppress and did not try to in his correspondence and in his one famous full-length book, *Notes on Virginia*. Written in 1782 and 1783, the book appeared in French, German, English and American editions during the next five years and made a great impression on the French political world, where liberals paid particular attention to the sections on the free institutions of republican government. The book has been said to have formulated principles of scientific geography later developed by von Humboldt, but the *Notes* also propagated the typical myths, slanders, notions and ideas, many of which are still current today.

Jefferson portrayed the Afro-American as being of inferior reason, incapable of ordinary mathematics, whose main aptitude appeared to be a musical capacity on the banjo. Whether the black would ever rise to the level of creating a full-scale musical composition Jefferson said he did not know. He elaborated on "the real distinctions which nature has made," and declared that there could be no solution through white and black living together except in the extermination of one or the other race. He theorized about color itself, reaching the conclusion that white was a beautiful color and that there was an "eternal monotony" in the countenance of the African. He described the hair and form of the white as more elegant and desirable than the similar physical characteristics of the African. He theorized on differences in the pulmonary apparatus of the Negro from that of the white, ventured into odors, and said, "Their existence appears to participate more of sensation than reflection. To this must be ascribed their disposition to sleep when abstracted from their diversions and unemployed in labor.

An animal whose body is at rest, and who does not reflect must be disposed to sleep of course." Borrowing from the taxonomists who studied dogs, cats, deer, he set down notions in the language of that science, "They are more ardent after their female, but love seems with them to be more an eager desire than a tender delicate mixture of sentiment and sensation. Their griefs are transient."

Jefferson set up his own dominoes, then knocked them over one at a time, demolishing the imported African for any use whatever except slavery—which he said he was opposed to. He declared that "in imagination they are dull, tasteless and anomalous." They forgot their troubles quicker than did the whites, and so on, and so on.

Such thinking was haled as scientific evaluation of the American Negro here and abroad. Jefferson concluded: "When freed, he is to be removed beyond the reach of mixture."

Benjamin Banneker, a Negro astronomer of Maryland, in 1791 sent a copy of *Banneker's Almanac* to Secretary of State Jefferson. In the *Almanac* he enclosed an eloquent letter which noted how inconsistent it was for Jefferson to raise so high the banner of freedom while owning slaves. Banneker wrote how pitiable it was for the author of lines like "all men are created equal" to detain human beings by fraud and violence. He urged Jefferson to look back on the American Revolution. "Suffer me to recall to your mind that time, in which the arms of the British crown were exerted, with every powerful effort in order to reduce you to a state of servitude . . . You were then impressed with proper ideas of the great violation of liberty, and the free possession of those blessings, to which you were entitled by nature; but, sir, how pitiable it is to reflect, that although you were so fully convinced of the benevolence of the Father of Mankind, and of his equal and impartial distribution of these rights and privileges which he hath conferred upon them, that you should at the same time counteract his mercies, in detaining by fraud and violence, so numerous a part of my brethren under groaning captivity and cruel oppression, that you should at the same time be found guilty of that most criminal act, which you professedly detested in others."

Answering Banneker, Jefferson, reflected upon the prospects of the black. "Nobody wishes more than I to see such proofs as you exhibit that Nature has given to our black brethren talents equal to those of other colors of men, and that the appearance of a want of them is owing merely to the degraded condition of their existence, both in Africa and America. I can add, with truth, that no one wishes more ardently to see a good system commenced for raising the condition of both their body and mind to what it ought to be, as fast as the imbecility of their present existence, and other circumstances which cannot be neglected, will admit."

In spite of Jefferson's attentive note to Banneker, he was in reality unconvinced. Later, in private correspondence, he belittled the mathematical and intellectual gifts of the almanac-maker.

Jefferson admired science perhaps more than all other realms. He had that admiration of science which the English master sometimes has for the mathematics expert. He had a keen interest in inventions, large or small; he was awed by Benjamin Franklin's scientific labors. He wrote of and glorified science.

He resented the statement of Count George L. de Buffon who had said, "One must be astonished that America has not yet produced a good poet, an able mathematician, a man of genius in a single art or single science." Jefferson replied to it in terms of the youth of our nation, and he made comparisons of our youth with the antiquity of European nations. He attributed the American lack of scientific knowledge to the fact that the United States had long been cut off from Great Britain by the Revolution. He found a dozen other reasons to explain why the United States—white, Anglo-Saxon America—had not culturally produced anything of note. But he was unable to see how the African, in the same and even a worse situation, stripped of *everything* and then enslaved, had failed to create.

Jefferson's foray into "racial science" reached its apogee when in 1815 he wrote to Francis Gray, a Massachusetts businessman, undertaking a mathematical description of race mixture. It delineated percentages of "white blood" and percentages of "Negro blood," measuring who could be free and who could not, according to such ancestral infusions. This theoretical spade work of Jefferson was one of the largest single contributions in the direction and actuality of racism.

Developments in natural science were now ready-made for followers of Jefferson to fall into the great wrap-up theory, the fixed idea of the three reigning races, Caucasoid, Mongoloid, Negroid. Last and least-human, of course, the Negroid.

Yet Jefferson was quite capable of making other observations of totally different character when he spoke of the way chattel slavery barbarized the white man's mind and soul.

"There must doubtless be an unhappy influence on the manners of our people produced by the existence of slavery among us," he wrote. "The whole commerce between master and slave is a perpetual exercise of the most boisterous passions, the most unremitting despotism on the one part, and degrading submissions on the other. Our children see this, and learn to imitate it; for man is an imitative animal. This quality is the germ of all education in him. From his cradle to his grave he is learning to do what he sees others do. The man must be a prodigy who can retain his manners and morals undepraved by such circumstances. And with what execration should the statesman be loaded, who, permitting one half the citizens thus to trample on the rights of the other, transforms those into despots, and these into enemies, destroys the morals of the one part, and the *amor patriae* of the other. For if a slave can have a country in this world, it must be any other in preference to that in which he is born to live and labor for another . . . Indeed I tremble for my country when I reflect that God is just; that his justice cannot sleep forever; that considering numbers, nature and natural means only, a revolution of the wheel of fortune, an exchange of situation is among possible events; that it may become probable by supernatural interference! The Almighty has no attribute which can take side with us in such a contest. But it is impossible to be temperate and to pursue this subject through the various considerations of policy, of morals, of history natural and civil. We must be contented to hope they will force their way into every one's mind. I think a change already perceptible, since the origin of the present revolution. The spirit of the master is abating, that of the slave rising from the dust, his condition mollifying, the way I hope preparing, under the auspices of heaven, for a total emancipation, and that this is disposed, in the order of events, to be with the consent of the masters, rather than by their extirpation."

Angels and demons certainly moved within the complex being of Mr. Jefferson.

ON TO THE CIVIL WAR

With the advent of the Nineteenth Century came two generations of intensified competition between the free labor and slave labor systems. Parallel with this was the struggle for possession of the mind. So many of our early Americans, leaders of the revolt from Britain, had by now an ingrained ambivalence in their souls. Their compromising gradualist hopes for emancipation, or more frequently colonization away from our soil, were mingled with strange intellectualizings about the essential nature of the slave. They beheld in color vast and impenetrable differences; a few even fancied the physical interior of the Negro as being virtually black blood, black bones, black intestines, "the pervading darkness."

Some, however, feared the effects of slavery on the white man.

The Virginia political leader, George Mason, suggested that slaveowning might affect the human mind itself, that slavery was a slow poison, that it influenced and contaminated the minds and morals of the slaveholders; he predicted that the drinking of that heady wine would pave the way for tyrannous legislation later on.

Patrick Henry, famous in every public school history book as having proclaimed, "Give me liberty or give me death," spoke as a white slaveholder. He disliked slavery and there is every evidence that he liked individual Negroes, as Jefferson and Washington had. But Patrick Henry had a plantation at Scotchtown on which there were thirty slaves. Once when a friend sent him an anti-slavery book written by a Frenchman, Henry expressed the contradiction of the time: "Every thinking honest man rejects slavery in Speculation, how few in practice? Would anyone believe that I am Master of slaves of my own purchase? I am drawn along by ye general Inconvenience of living without them; I will not, I cannot justify it."

After the Missouri Compromise, Secretary of State John Quincy Adams talked about the effect of slavery upon the minds of the white. He said that the Missouri Question betrayed the secret of the slaveholders' souls. In the abstract they admitted that slavery was an evil, they disclaimed all participation in the introduction of it and cast it all upon the shoulders of Britain. But when probed to the quick upon it, said Adams, they showed at the bottom of their souls pride and vainglory in their condition of masterdom. They fancied themselves more generous and noble-hearted than the plain freemen who labored for subsistence. They looked down upon the simplicity of a Yankee's manners, because he had not habits of overbearing like theirs and could not treat Negroes like dogs.

"It is among the evils of slavery that it taints the very sources of moral principles," Adams said. "It establishes false estimates of virtue and vice; for what can be more false and heartless than this doctrine which makes the first and holiest rights of humanity to depend upon the color of the skin."

John Sergeant, Pennsylvania member of Congress, opposing the extension of slavery into Missouri, spoke on the pernicious effect of slavery upon the mind. It was incisive perception on the pride-generating process. "Let every man who has been accustomed to the indulgence of being a slaveholder ask himself if it is not a luxury—a tempting luxury, which solicits him strongly at every moment. The prompt obedience, the ready attention, the submissive and humble, but eager effort to anticipate command—how flattering to our pride, how soothing to our indolence!"

Frances Trollope, the Englishwoman who lived in this country for a while in the 1820s, at a time when the plantation economy spread and "the making of the

South" was intensively on, wrote *Domestic Manners of the Americans.* In it she observed the effect of slavery upon white morality. She related the story of a small slavegirl who had mistakenly eaten bread and butter containing arsenic, which had been intended for poisoning rats. She remarked that the idea of really sympathising in the sufferings of the slavegirl appeared to her masters and mistresses as absurd as weeping over a calf that had been slaughtered by the butcher. Mrs. Trollope noted how economic condition transmogrified white psychology into something grotesquely other than nature had intended: "Among the poorer class of landholders, who are often as profoundly ignorant as the negroes they own, the effect of this plenary power over males and females is most demoralising; and the kind of coarse, not to say brutal, authority which is exercised, furnishes the most disgusting moral spectacle I ever witnessed. In all ranks, however, it appeared to me that the greatest and best feelings of the human heart were paralysed by the relative positions of slave and owner. The characters, the hearts of children are irretrievably injured by it."

By the 1820s and 1830s the slave was so depressed as a consequence of an array of speculative, religious, political, pseudo-scientific and practical walls that he was powerless and virtually dependent for any moral support upon white antislavers. His only outlets were usually abortive local uprisings, and there were several of consequence, individual acts of retaliation against harsh masters and flight to the North. In numerous Southern states there were antislavery organizations of a local character, but a new upsurge of aggressive proslavery groups had the effect of driving them out of existence or into an inefficacious underground.

Another force, the parliamentary-political-philosophic authority of the slave power in Congress and in other phases of Federal Government, became assertive and threatening. Preeminent spokesman of this parliamentary power was John C. Calhoun. He lived in a special, personal image of himself as a great Athenian orator, a modern Pericles, and he had the support of planters and slaveholders. Basically Calhoun tried to make his appeal to other parliamentarians, to the uncommitted, even to antislavery advocates. In the Senate men tried to make converts one of the other; their speeches went into the record and the press and they influenced the citizenry. Calhoun was expert; he was in the tradition of Jefferson and Madison, and in addition a very practical politician. He loved the Union, but he loved slavery more.

His impact was as an advocate of states rights. Mainly he believed that there was a class of "betters" who must rule and they should not have to work. In return for running government, free workmen and slaves ought to be grateful to their "betters" because they would be well taken care of.

For a rationalization of slavery he went to the ancient political aristocracy of Greece. He viewed Greek civilization as the ultimate desideratum. He likened slaveocracy in its potential to the aristocracy that had once characterised Athens. He called the slave institution a "positive good." Slaves were well-treated and white masters kind. The master-slave relationship formed the most solid and durable foundation on which to rear free and stable political institutions. Inequality was the natural state of man, it had been so in all ages. He asked Northern parliamentarians and businessmen to unite with him and the planters against rising laboring and mercantile groups in the North. He told Josiah Quincy that "the interests of gentlemen of the North and of the South are identical." His position forecast the famous North-South alliance of conservatives which would develop later, but not until 1876.

Calhoun's writings and his speeches in the Senate, his prestige as a former Secretary of State, taken in combination with his frequent iteration of these aristocratic Greek-Republic positions, influenced and dominated all Southern parliamentarians. His philosophy spread over the South and it helped confirm Northern proslavery whites.

Calhoun argued that slavery could make good loyal Americans out of all white men because of that one thing they had in common—the color of their skin. He told John Quincy Adams that the best guarantee of equality among the whites was slavery because it produced an unvarying level among whites and it did not even admit of inequalities by which one white man could domineer another. There was truth in this, for that was the way it worked out. Poor whites, recognizing that they had some status and were not all the way at the bottom, hardened their attitude about blacks and stayed "on the right side." Upperclass whites, to secure the support of the poorer ones, displayed a commonalty of feeling for the poorer whites that was altogether different from their attitude toward slaves.

Calhoun affected especially the small man's thinking, stimulating him to admire planters and slaveholders. The little man, often ambitious, anxious to improve his status, altered his view to assume the new outlook of those who had "arrived." It was the thing to do, to be. It was socially acceptable. Such appeals affected Northerners as well as Southerners. William Lloyd Garrison saw how the sweep of the slaving mentality penetrated New England minds. In the first issue of *The Liberator,* he wrote that the New England brain was a menace, containing a "contempt more bitter, opposition more active, detraction more relentless, prejudice more stubborn, and apathy more frozen than among slaveowners themselves."

In helping to generate that mentality, or to solidify what was already there, to shape and strengthen the so-called "color curtain," Calhoun was an effectual contributor.

Many observers at home and some from abroad were aware that the African had been transformed in the New World, but one visitor to America noticed how the white man had become altered. This was the famous French author, Count Alexis de Tocqueville, who spent several years on American soil at about the time Calhoun's oratory and impact was at its height. De Tocqueville has since become—and deservedly—the darling of many historians of the first half of the 19th century. Many of his perceptive observations on the nature of the white American hold true today.

The all-white-equal concept that John C. Calhoun tried to generate de Tocqueville saw as already operating. He beheld how a common alliance against the black bred a socialization of interest among all of the ex-Europeans. He remarked that in Europe rich and poor were at pains to keep separate, but here, *interest,* the common interest, united them on at least one point, superiority over the black. There was a floor beneath which no white man could go politically and that floor was the Negro's ceiling.

But this visitor observed that as a consequence of slave labor there were numerous classes of whites, especially in the South, who regarded all labor as a sign of inferiority. Slaves work, therefore work is to be shunned, because slaves are to be shunned. If slaves were debased and labor was what debased them, stay away from labor. As a result an idling, parasitic class developed. Gamblers, romantics, dandies, drinkers made their appearance and with many their only creative claim was that they weren't black.

De Tocqueville remarked that slavery degraded the black population, but it enervated the white, and while its fatal effects were recognized by both groups, still the system was preserved. He said that it threatened the future of those who maintained it and it ruined the State, but it had become part of the habits and prejudices of the colonists. He reached the conclusion that the condition of the master class was the best proof of all that slavery was not made for man.

He had, in his own way, remarked on the same "boisterous extravagance of the nature of mastery" which Jefferson had noted. Out of all this came the mouldy flower of chivalry, the country gentleman, the charming and neurotic white ladies of the big house, the mint-julep aristocrat, the fun of the hunt, the expert on horses, the minuet, the wine cellar, foppery, dudery, pretensions to sophistication, idleness—all the trappings of the so-called Athenian life of the Southern plantation. De Tocqueville thought it was sad and deteriorative: the human nature he saw among the white masters impressed him as a distortion of all natural value.

"If it be true that each people has a special character independent of its political interest," he said, "just as each man has one independent of his social position, one might say that America gives the most perfect picture, for good and for ill, of the special character of the English race. The American is the Englishman left to himself." And he enumerated: "Spirit coldly burning, serious, tenacious, selfish, cold, frozen imagination, having respect for money, industrious, proud and rationalist."

He had pictured the nature of white domination. Even the prophetic de Tocqueville couldn't know that it would persevere long after one of the worst civil wars in history.

The Negro slave in America saw around him a free, burgeoning world, alive with excitement, energy and limitless horizons—for others.

The needs of the American continent stimulated science and invention and led to new ways of harnessing a raw world. Steam power resulted in a new way of looking at what could be done with ships and factories. More than two hundred steamboats were running in our rivers by 1830. By 1840 the building of railroads was begun in the North and the South. The invention of Eli Whitney of the cotton engine infused new life into the slave institution. The cotton gin, a form of mass handling of raw cotton, drove the South to cultivate more cotton and to find and fetter more slaves. New England and England bought the product, and the manufacture of cotton into cloth and other products put new productive forces into motion here and in England. With cotton wealth and energy expanding, a vital industry in modern countries, banking, took on growth. Banking and industrial manufacture, followed by exports, produced problems of tariff between our country and the Old World. As these developments occurred, as the cotton kingdom spread along the Gulf States, as modern-style factories operated by wage-workers sprang up in the North, Federal Government became more complicated. In Washington each new Administration had to face the complex situation of the slavery economic interest contraposed to the business and wage labor economy that spread over New York State, Pennsylvania and all the New England States, and later the Western States.

Governments and people in Europe saw a large contradiction in the way our society was shaping up. They were aware that the United States was something new in the world, a "great experiment" was underway; America was theoretically the home of new thinking, free experimental ways; there was good land to live on and room enough for varieties of ideas to be worked out. But they also saw that we held onto chattel slavery more fiercely than any other country in the New World. We had fought off England and set off liberation waves in other parts of the world. Serfs and slaves were being emancipated, all over the world, but not in this boiling land of America where so much "liberty of spirit" seemed prevalent. By the 1830s it was clear that chattel slavery was battening down for a long stay, perhaps forever. This spectacle implemented the contradiction of a growing, feverish, expanding, power-generating land which ought to be consistent about its free democratic principles, but was not.

Other countries were liberating black slaves and white serfs. Argentina in 1810 promulgated a law freeing the children of all slaves. In 1814 the Mexican Congress issued a Declaration of Independence along the lines prepared by Jefferson and freed its slaves, and about fifteen years later, because it was necessary, Mexico reaffirmed the liberation of slaves. In the next decade one South American nation after another took the same path: Colombia, Peru, Bolivia.

By 1855 there were only three slave areas left in the Western Hemisphere: Cuba, Brazil, and the United States. Britain had tossed slavery out of its dominions by 1833. In Russia there was a great stirring to get the serf-peasants out of bondage. The liberal spirit of the Nineteenth Century was for freedom, except in the expanding United States where the slave power was racing westward and planting cotton and slavery as it moved.

The biggest economic problem has always been to secure the most production for the least cost. This was clearly and early recognized by New England manufacturers in the textile field. During the second decade of the

Nineteenth Century the world's first full-scale factories for the complete manufacture of cotton into cloth were established in Boston, Waltham and other New England cities. This led to a search for new kinds of labor and new ways of employing labor and keeping it happy at small wages.

All industry joined the search for more and cheaper mass production, for ways to can food, to make engines for all kinds of purposes, to put motors into whatever could be motor-driven. Owners who made profits often put them back into plant expansion and new machinery. Leather manufacture and wagon manufacture became big industries.

But little of this was experienced in the South. It was a world of its own. Most work was done by hand, the slave's hand. Slaves built the houses, served the white people, drove their carriages, ploughed their fields; as in the North everything moved more and more on wheels.

Inventors were already at work on contraptions which sought to find the secret of perpetual motion. Getting a good invention on the market was the way to riches. The best Yankee minds watched the developments in the field of electricity in England and elsewhere. Steam power became wedded to the engine, young people experimented with a marvel called photography. Most of this inquiry was in the North and in New England. The whole practice was to have the effect of erecting an industrial free-labor society in that part of the country. Migrants from the North who moved westward took with them this spirit of the engine, the factory, the machine.

But the South was something else—the cumbersome empire that Calhoun said was stately, supreme and founded on slave labor. Even then it began to look antedated against the big cities in the cooler part of the nation where commerce, industry, science and invention and money madness ruled. New York City, by 1830, was the country's foremost economic center. Even in cotton production forty percent on each dollar ended up in that city.

The machine became the new god of the new people. With machines you could build six-story skyscrapers such as they had in New York, boats to go on the canals; and only machines could make the wheels, engines and coaches that were necessary to the all-vital growing railroad industry.

Clearly one kind of America was being built in the upper regions of the country and another kind was persisting below the Mason-Dixon line. Beyond the economic and industrial features the people themselves were different in each section. Their values differed.

It was an event for northern residents to take a one or two months' coach ride south to see slavery at first hand. It was an event for slaveholders to go north and to witness the excitement of the big cities, the changing urban scene, the faster motion in the streets.

America was changing. And dividing.

Negroes were now cast into two groups, free Negroes and the slaves. Some free Negroes had been liberated through service in the American Revolution and their sons and daughters were free also. They were located mainly in the North. Their "free" status was, to be truthful, limited. They occupied a secondary position, for they did the menial work chiefly, housework, field work, sanitation work, but they were in a struggle with society to become mechanics. To become expert in some mechanical way was to become part free in reality. Free Negroes often participated in the growing antislavery movement in New England. Some became widely known as articulate Abolitionists. A few sought to gain status by efforts in literature and the arts but the odds against them were overwhelming.

From Delaware to Texas, the slave was in a cage. He must labor, carry identification passes, say yessir to all whites, bow, keep quiet and not revolt. He could get his foot into the Bible but that was about all. For the rest he must produce the rice, sugar, cotton, tobacco that the South thrived on. Most slaves lived on plantations, but some lived in the small towns of the South. The ones on the plantations had the harder life.

The great lie propagated about them was best expressed by a Virginia lawyer, George Fitzhugh, who stated in a book called *Cannibals All* that the slaves of the South were the happiest and in some sense the freest people in the world. The children and the aged and infirm worked not at all, and yet they had all the comforts and necessities of life provided for them. They enjoyed liberty, he said, because they were oppressed neither by care nor by labor.

This concept was propagated everywhere and it found its way into the sweet Southern songs like *Dixie*.

The slave who had a specialty he could perform was in better shape than the plantation hand. As carpenter, blacksmith, leather designer, basket maker, furniture maker, or some similar trade, he received better treatment than the black who labored in the cotton and the sun. House slaves who ministered to the wants of the family were more favored. These variations of role of the slaves made for a minor caste system inside their own framework. Being a free Negro meant something; being of lighter color meant even more; being a house slave was a notch higher than picking cotton.

Slaves and free Negroes had a world and a means of communication of their own. They helped fugitives to escape to the North; sometimes they banded together and undertook a bitter uprising. But by and large they were so bound to the master that they could not unite and organize.

The Negroes could not get together for any general rising because the law was rigid and the enforcement more rigid. Groups larger than three or four couldn't congregate; they couldn't carry arms. They weren't allowed to signal each other with drums, song, or any other communication; but even so the whites were sometimes outwitted. The police system throughout the South was well regulated. Mounted patrols visited slave quarters. Every white man was expected to serve in a local militia to keep an eye on the black. Curfews existed in every town.

While the South kept tabs on its labor supply, the North was tinkering with metals to get robot mechanisms to replace slave labor and even free labor. Metallurgy, chemistry, all crafts pertaining to harnessing mineral and natural resources—these became the pursuits of northern business. In the North they chased after iron, coal, copper, silver, gold, nickel, everything that could come out of the earth and be converted into mechanisms to replace human labor and to assist humans in their harder chores. From 1800 to 1850 the most aspiring money makers in the North put their brains and hands to making the earth yield more profitable items than cotton and tobacco. In this period the South took on much of the agricultural character that it has now, and the North the industrial character that it retained into the next century. These differences, the industrial system versus the plantation system, made all the difference only a few years later.

As for Negroes, free and slave alike, they must wait. A great and complex society was breaking up around them as a result of irreconcilable social and economic forces. Yet the Negro himself, lowly as his status might be, was the leading, catalytic factor.

In the three or four decades before the Civil War there

was a rapid convergence of new forces in the North. Migration to the West increased; millions entered the country from Europe; New York City grew as a commercial center and port; the Erie Canal was built and it accelerated all commerce between New England, New York and the mid-West; and the telegraph was invented. No one could clearly foretell how such developments would re-shape the political picture, nor could anyone foresee how at last there would loom two clashing systems —the slave labor interest in contraposition to the free labor society.

In the North there were chronic contests to build a political form which would encompass bursting economic and industrial needs. Parties came and went. An early Republican Party faded out and a Whig Party arose. The Whigs split into northern and southern factions. A Liberal Party arose; then a Free Soil force. Behind the scenes a man named Thurlow Weed, the first of an unending procession of political "dictators" managed to name several Presidents. In 1856 his candidate for the Presidency, General Fremont, was defeated, and thereafter he began grooming one of the most famous antislavers and statesmen, William H. Seward.

In 1849 gold had been discovered in California and the slave issue arose. Would that State come into the Union as a slave state or as a free state? This became a debate in Congress; at the heart of the debate was the same blunt and simple matter that rankled the nation since its founding: the manhood of the black man. Was the nation to go on forever keeping him debased, or would he, in California, have a chance to be all-man?

Seward, in an address in the United States Senate on *Freedom in the New Territories,* opposing the admission of California into the Union as a slave state, went back to the Constitution, as all principled arguments in our country do. He went to John Jay, an antislaver, who had suggested in *The Federalist* how slavery should be handled in the Constitution. "Let the case of the slaves be considered, as in truth a peculiar one. Let the compromising expedient of the Constitution be mutually adopted which regards them as *inhabitants,* but as debased below the equal level of free inhabitants, which regards the slaves as divested of two-fifths of the man."

Was it possible, Seward asked, that in this new world, with its dedication to free principles, we could openly promulgate as a legal and philosophic principle that men, that a man anywhere, could be so divested? Nevertheless, he said, this left three-fifths of a man, a person, a living, breathing, moving, reasoning man.

Seward went on to say: "The right to *have* a slave implies the right in some one to *make* the slave."

A great implication flowed from this. If men or slaves had been *made,* and law and a thousand instruments of force had manufactured them, then such men, slaves, could also be unmade, de-invented as it were. It might take a supreme effort to set the wheels into reverse—the wheels of war itself: and this whole period, and Seward and his statements in particular, graphed these possibilities.

The force with which a whole nation had for centuries crushed a human segment had gone as far as it could. There is apparently a trait in the political-historical nature of man that he can remain in slavery only so long; and then from somewhere, in him or in others, machinery of reversal goes into motion. That was the stark situation of the nation's life in the 1950s. All forces were synergistic, moving toward an irrepressible meeting.

Our history from 1800 on as written presented the glories of American achievements as exclusively white accomplishments. Only Caucasians built civilizations; only white culture amounted to anything.

History and historians achieved this effect by ignoring the existence of the Negro as he had been ignored or spliced up in the Constitution, or treating him as the happy-go-lucky national banjo player who incidently worked all day for nothing.

A few years after the Revolutionary War, historians and educators, working in the early public and private schools, began the teaching of a nationalism and conservatism. We had a baptism in fire to work with, a tradition: we had founding Fathers, a Constitution, and even a Father of the Country. We had the apostle of modern time, Benjamin Franklin.

A Kentuckian, Robert J. Breckenridge, in *Formation and Development of the American Mind,* published in 1847, wrote that the destiny of America was to spread the great ideas of the day, to elevate and improve the individual, to teach man to govern himself, to love his fellowman, to love his God, to teach the nations that all men were equal, to revere human rights, to raise up the downtrodden.

A poetry of American nationalism had begun as far back as Philip Freneau in the prior century; by the mid-1830s there was an established and growing white-oriented drum-beating glory literature. To counterbalance this there were only the dawning expressions of the anti-slavers and the Abolitionists. The success of *Uncle Tom's Cabin* was a notable exception to the general literary and historical process. What to us is sentimental and contrived in that familiar story was a glimpse of reality and guilt to millions of that day.

The term Jim Crow first began to be heard.

In the 1840's and '50s, the slaves groaned on their plantations, perhaps not even knowing that in the white overreaches of the North and South such a flood of national sentiment and grandiose verbiage flowed like banners in a coming wind. Annually the whites celebrated the Fourth of July with increasing fervor while the black masses wondered what they had to celebrate. A holiday like Thanksgiving Day spilled over onto the plantations —but thank whom for what? Christmas alone became the holiday of truce between the whites and the black masses. Anything having to do with the chink in the white man's armor—his religion, his *profession* of Christianity—the Negro seized upon, for it was the first, the most available rung on his ladder upward.

Intellectuals of every stamp willingly, zealously, carried on the burden of selling the white man's glory. Many of their books lent credence to the picture and actuality of white power, and by omission, of black virtual nonexistence as people, as citizens.

Titles by the hundreds, from then into present times, concealed this white-racial narcissism: *The American Mind, The Making of an American, The American Conscience, The Cultural Life of the Colonies, The Great Awakening.* These and similar titles filled the stacks of American libraries. But it cannot be forgotten that they were all excessively oriented to the white race—the white mind, white America, white conscience and culture and white awakening. We fostered an approach to historiography and national background that treated our national role as liberal, benevolent, democratic, tolerant, humanitarian and just. All of these attributes referred to white America. The black man had no role.

However objective and scholarly he considered himself, the average historian of that day, born and reared in all-white communities, virtually did not know that

Negroes existed as human beings. The only *people* were
the whites: of these he sang; these he studied, delineated,
fashioned into his pages. If he discussed the making of
the American mind, he meant the Anglo or European-
originated mind. If he spoke of national conscience he
meant white conscience about white issues. If he described national heroes he meant white heroes. He wrote
of the founding period in hallowed terms, evolving an
arsenal of expressions: the American way, or dream or
heritage, or creed of liberty. He arrogated to the soil
between Canada and Mexico and between the two
oceans the name American.

Such effusions poured over and around the Negro in
such quantity that he was in danger of drowning in a sea
of confusion, not knowing clearly whether this was
worked for or against him. At the last he discovered that
most of this had been white men talking to white men.
From the root days he had been told that he was three-
fifths of a man. There was a high frequency for whites and
a lower one for blacks. On the lower frequency the truths
of his real condition and his relation to the overworld
came at him in a thousand daily ways including the
books, anthems, Congressional speeches and newspapers.

Thus even in the historical records, two psychologies
generated side by side, one with its high idealistic confidence in the grandeur of the land, and the other a private
realization of life inside a myth within an illusion inside a
nightmare.

The Muse of History as recorded in that era may have
worked the meanest unkindness of all upon the black
subject. For history at least is supposed to tell the
truth.

The pseudo-science of race, off to a start in the time of Jefferson, was by the 1850s a thriving, circulating, powerfully mind-influencing phenomenon. It twined around the body and soul of the Negro like a boa constrictor. In a time when the word "science" began to be worshipped, more in the United States than anywhere else in the world, articulate hedonists of white superiority cloaked themselves in the mantle of supposed "new learning" to justify racist formulae and theories.

The monster of racial alienation has existed—often unrecognized—in the history of man for millennia. Whether as caste in India or as class in Europe, as warlord and serf in China, or as Super-race and Sub-race in the United States, this sociological brew was composed of strange ingredients—of fantasy and witchcraft, property and money, superstition, religion, fear, blood, self-interest, consanguinity, murder, power, alienation and God-reaching. Its fumes wafted in the breezes of the medieval world, notably in the central and northern regions of Europe. It was there in Wotan and Siegfried, the Vikings, in folk heroes; it had been among the Greeks in their gods, great gods and lesser gods.

From about the Sixteenth Century until the beginnings of the present century, the brew of race mixed and stewed in the form of steadily intensifying nationalisms. In an area that ranged from England to the Continent, to Germany, France, north to the Scandinavian countries, there became increasingly an awareness of pigment and hair as worth having significance. Western and Northern Europe, aware that it was mechanically, industrially, and artistically ahead of other continents, began to attribute the inventions and creations of the few to the mores and biological characteristics of the many. They began to generate pride, to inflate with nationalism. They contrasted European culture with the primal backgrounds of other continents and simplicities of other distant, primitive peoples. Still, in none of Europe's tongues in earlier centuries did they use the word race or have any such word with its contemporary connotations.

The term emerged in modern times in the Italian *razza;* then passed into the French language as *race.* From there it entered the English language. With Linneaus it acquired natural science uses.

From there, as an application to the divisions and the alienations of the world's humans, the term made a precipitate entrance into the rhetoric of American and English statesmen after the Revolutionary War.

Blood kinship became a matter of political consequence. It was affirmed even in our Declaration of Independence in Jefferson's words of appeal to the English: ". . . we have conjured them by the ties of our common kindred . . . They too have been deaf to the voice of justice and consanguinity."

Jefferson remarked the fact that in one hundred and fifty years of American settlement the realm of theory and research had not taken a look at the nature of the red man nor of the black. Nor was there any science of anthropology as yet which looked at white men either. But because of Jefferson's stimulation, because an age of inquiry was opening and because racial rationalization began to make its appearance as a national or sectional need, that lag ended.

By the mid 1800s and throughout the Civil War, a complete front of racial-intellectual ideology-making was in great tide.

Dr. Samuel G. Morton, a Philadelphia physician, set out in the 1830s to measure head sizes of various ethnic types. Gathering charts, tables, graphs, drawings of the human physiognomy seemed to Morton the way to develop a science of human beings. Mixed with the gathering of such data was the hypothesis that the size of the head determined brain capacity and the extent of human faculty and creativity. Individuals were superior, he believed, as their skulls were larger.

Neurology of the present may have some of its origins in portions of the investigative work of that time. But the unfortunate fact is that the political ethnologists who worked from predispositions about what they wanted to prove mainly handled their data in ways to support the slavocracy. Ethnological ideas settled into two general concepts: one, that man was a single species, a single human family; and the other was a concept of plurality that broke up mankind into varieties of order, with differences of capacity and quality.

The word race began to make its appearance in book titles around the time Dr. Morton began taking head measurements. Charles Caldwell published *Thoughts on the Unity of the Human Race* in 1830. The titles came closer to their purpose in another book appearing in 1845, Josiah Priest's *Slavery as It Relates to the Negro Race*.

More influential than the others was the work of Dr. Josiah C. Nott, a congenital Democrat Southerner, whose *Collections on the Natural History of the Caucasian and Negro Races* was published at Mobile, Alabama in 1844. That work was an important demarcation point in the processes of theoretical race-making in our national life.

It had taken two and one-quarter centuries, beginning with the time the first Negroes arrived as servants or slaves in Virginia, for this title and theme to make its appearance. It required that long for a clearcut so-called Caucasian and clearcut so-called Negro to be developed or divided on American soil and to warrant, at this time, academic and professional imprimatur. By carefully looking at teeth, muscles, color, hair, Nott piled up a huge book-sized awareness of differentiation among peoples which was supposed to be relevant, important, decisive, final.

Working in Alabama with a black and mulatto population, seeing the slaves in the cotton fields, meeting and living with the plantation owners he knew and liked, Nott made observations that proved conclusively, so he said, that the black man was little above the level of an ape. All of his contrasts and comparisons with the superior Caucasian led him to reiterative pictures of the slave as an inferior figure naturally destined to his servile role, specifically designed for slavery.

Dr. Nott, along with C. R. Gliddon, in 1844, published an all-embracing book filled with graphs, cartoons, figures of the human physiognomy. In this work the black emerged at the bottom of the human scale; the yellow man fared not much better; the red man fared badly; but the white emerged as upright, courageous, noble, intelligent. This large tome appeared at a time when the planters needed a strong reply to arguments of Northern antislavers.

Dr. Nott's views spread to northern conservative intellectuals. So permeative was the racist wash of that day that it even produced a scientific myopia in the famous Louis Agassiz. Agassiz supported Nott's depiction of black and white variation.

The competition among ethnologists to establish a natural and an eternal subhuman level for the black man led Dr. Samuel A. Cartwright, a Louisianian, to claim in 1852, in his *Slavery in the Light of Ethnology,* that pigmentation went inside the colored person, to the membranes, the tendons, the muscles; and it colored even the fluids and the secretions. Cartwright wrote: "Even the negro's brain and nerves, the chyle and all the humors are tinctured with the shade of the pervading darkness."

But it was Dr. Nott, headquartered in the deepest part of the Deep South, who remained the energizing figure in the psuedo-intellectual racist movement. He kept in touch with developments in Europe on what came to be known as "the race front," for counterparts and prototypes of the American school flourished abroad.

A Frenchman, Count Arthur de Gobineau, wrote a book called the *Inequality of the Human Races*. Nott wrote the introduction for this one and prepared the appendix. In 1856, when the American debate on slavery was reaching the level of national crisis, Count de Gobineau's work, translated into English, was issued at Philadelphia.

De Gobineau was a Germanophile who believed that Teutons, alternately called Aryans, should rule the world. The Frenchman made use of the anti-Negro findings of his American colleagues. His total philosophy took its departure from alleged black inferiority and his prime laboratory was the experience in the United States.

Count de Gobineau's notions divided the races of the world into white, yellow and black, a division suggested by others. He theorised that this segmentation of man overshadowed all other problems in history. His whites were the Nordics. The Alpines were yellow and Asiatic in origin. The Mediterraneans were of black or African origin. He viewed Semites and Mediterraneans as a chaos which had been a transmission belt of "African blood."

De Gobineau subscribed to the head size theory of Dr. Morton and other ethnologists and borrowed from Morton's measurements to prove that the large head size of Caucasians meant more brains and more human worth.

As some contradictions to this notion had appeared in the observations of others, Dr. Nott told his readers: "I accordingly applied to three hat dealers in Mobile, and a large manufacturer in New Jersey, for statement of the relative number of hats of each size sold to adult males. Their tables agree so perfectly as to leave no doubt as to the circumference of the heads of the white population of the United States. The three houses together disposed of about 15,000 hats annually."

It was a fine lot of hats. But hardly a scientific measurement of the mind of America, white or black.

Count de Gobineau, using the "researches" of Americans, reached the conclusion: "The dark races are the lowest on the scale. The shape of the pelvis has a character of animalism, which is imprinted in the individuality of that race ere their birth, and seems to portend their destiny."

In the United States, believers in slavery, looking for any and all rationalization that would help keep their system afloat, quoted as authorities men like Nott, Morton and de Gobineau. The Frenchman generalized: "Some of his (the Negro's) senses have an acuteness unknown to the other races, the sense of taste and that of smell, for instance . . . But it is precisely this development of the animal faculties that stamps the Negro with the mark of inferority." To confirm this, Nott pointed out that he knew of Negroes around Mobile who ate fox, crocodiles and other animals that whites wouldn't touch. "I am aware," he wrote, "that some persons north of the Mason and Dixon line might be disposed to explain this by asserting that hunger drove them to such extremities but I can testify from my own observation that this is not the case."

Publicists throughout the South, even in the North, borrowed from these asserted findings, repeated and improved upon them. The *Texas Almanac,* which reached farmhouses throughout the South, in 1857 popularized and sought to justify this thinking: ". . . because the African is an inferior being, differently organized from the white man, with wool instead of hair on his head— with lungs, feet, joints, lips, nose and cranium so distinct as to indicate a different and inferior grade of being."

It was this kind of "science" that filled the air of the 1840s and 1850s, and as the clashing sections of the country sought to defend their positions, the race researchers became vital in the Southern cause. These figures by now replaced the theologians as the intellectual and spiritual prestige center. They replaced the Calhoun-style thinkers who talked of the South as the grand Athenian Republic. Now the Notts and the Mortons were bulwarked by a French nobleman. From that period on there occurred an unending transfer, back and forth, between the United States and Europe of racist theorizings.

It was to take only another fifty years for de Gobineau societies to flourish as a precursor to Hitlerism.

The graphic term *power structure* is of recent vintage, seized upon by the modern civil rights movement in its struggle to grasp a hold upon oppressive Government. Of course the power structure originated in the colonial commerce; it accelerated in the time of the founding of the nation; by the 1850s the power structure was a ponderous but divided force. The head-on collision of the slave empire against the free-labor business-enterprise forces within Federal Government was mainly in evidence in the policy conflicts of the United States Congress. The struggles of the 1850s over policy, mostly on the carving up of the West into segments free or slave, confirmed the crystallization of national centralized struggle of factions of great strength.

By the 1850s it was clear that there were two power blocs, and that one, the Northern, was committed in a vague way against slavery and was somehow on the side of the slave. From the time of the battle over the admission of California and the passage of the Fugitive Slave Act in 1850, Union preservation emerged as the massive issue of the time. If the Union could be preserved, one single Federal power structure could hold the nation together. If it sundered, two hostile nations might emerge on American soil, a Southern slave nation, a Northern industrial nation. The forces of empire coalescing and advancing in the North only signified all the more—in the color-line reasoning which had become a mode of national thinking—how all-powerful was the Caucasian, with his industry, science, ecological spread, his machines, his mechanical emancipation. All through the 1800s, as shiploads of slaves arrived from tribal Africa and as these new spectators beheld the marvels and powers of the American scene, the trains, telegraph, the dawning mass production, the whole developing magic of the new materialism—all through this, the new arrivals as well as the already "Americanized" slaves and free Negroes, saw power and more power rearing over and about them: the effect was to create a strange Negro respect for the ways of this world along with a realization of the enormity of the burden of throwing off the accumulating weight of the yoke which the slave system of economics imposed. How was it to be done? Who could do it?

The power structure, now a divided force, had been building toward disintegration ever since the national outlines were limned in the compromise Constitution. Abolitionists, anti-slavers, free-soilers who favored settle-

ment of the West as free territory, and ambitious industrialists who wanted to see the whole land released from
the grip of the slave system were caught up in a battering-
ram process destined to demolish the Southern economy.
Abolitionists who had been fighting the slave institution
since about 1800 resolved into a few positions. The followers of William Lloyd Garrison held a simple and
rather strange position: dissolve the Union, let the South
go its own way and let the North be free. This position,
essentially moralist, denounced the Constitution itself as
a covenant with the forces of disaster. It failed to think
out matters in terms of ultimate national destiny; it did
not plan in such terms: it simply called for dissolution.

The theory of "colonization" found advocates from
the time of Thomas Jefferson or before. Send them back
to Africa, or export them to the West Indies; ship them
out, in any case. Remove the blot. Buy off the slaveholders; pay them for each slave, transport them back to the
nearest available jungles. That policy even resulted in the
formation in the 1840s of the West African nation Liberia, composed of and settled by Afro-Americans
shipped back to Africa; and this policy even gripped Lincoln later at the outset of the Civil War as the likeliest
solution.

Advocates of parliamentary political action against
slavery visualised the importance of stopping slavery
from extending westward. These became the liberal free-
soil advocates. Let slavery stop at Kansas, they said. Let
it not spread into California, they argued. This voice on
official levels carried the major burden of social change
of that time; it produced the most significant confronta-
tion between Northern and Southern politicians, statesmen, legislatures.

Yet there was also a wing of violence within the antislavery forces. Militants of the John Brown stripe be-

lieved that only by the shedding of blood would it be possible to resolve the slave issue. Brown worked toward setting up black and white rule upon an equal basis; he commanded a small military group with which he hoped to bring about his objectives. Slaves would rise and fight if they were armed, he believed. Black and white together could seize arsenals, overthrow States, cities, the Government itself. In all ages of man there have been such militants on the side of the oppressed. Brown represented the outermost militant interest identified with black emancipation.

The most sensible opponents of slavery were possibly the parliamentary politicals, those who believed that Government itself must be stocked with the right men, the right policies, and that law backed by force and public respect must ultimately bring about desired progress.

One figure, black, unknown and unappreciated by modern America to this day, a figure of prophetic grandeur, emerged as a titan of sound reason, common sense and militant initiative. This was Frederick Douglass who, arriving in the North in the 1840s, had by 1850 guided the antislavery movement so intelligently that it was able to become an underriding force in the development of the Republican Party. This guidance emerged inside the Republican Party as an unseen rudder which perhaps more than any other factor in the land drove Abraham Lincoln toward his emancipation policy. Douglass, whose tone, language and action was on the order of that of the Founding Revolutionists of 1776, a man of the stature of Washington, Adams or Jefferson, rose to a level of eloquence and personal initiative whereby his books, his newspapers, his oratory, his influence upon all personalities in Northern politics became of determining significance. Douglass remains in the shadowed backwash of American statesmenship, for precisely the same

reason that his people remain in the American shadow
world. His autobiography, one of the most appealing political documents in American history, recounts a life of
long political activity powerfully and sensibly leading his
people toward a position of exerting decisive influence
during the Civil War.

Douglass dominated the antislavery movement in the
1850s; he taught hundreds of thousands of Northerners
how morally, ethically and economically they might and
ought to oppose the slave institution.

Douglass beheld in Christianity itself the major contradiction of the New World, and of its conflict of policy
over slavery. From the time the slaves had been brought
here under the rationale that they were being kidnaped
to save their souls, black men and women had learned
that this was the chink in the armor of the Caucasian.
The white man claimed to be a Christian, but enslaved
the black. Let this a-moral contradiction be hurled back
at the white man day after day through all the generations of slavery. So Douglass and his black followers decided. And this they set out to do.

Douglass lectured. He wrote words of defiance in his
publication *The North Star*. From the Bible itself he
seized verbal grenades to hurl at North and South, friend
and foe: "We will continue to make drafts upon the
Bible," he said, "in order to wage the war against slavery." Douglass held high the gonfalon of Biblical contradiction, as Martin Luther King and others hold it high in
our own day, and used the Bible's teachings to refute
chattel slavery and rebuff Christian pretense. He utilized
moral, political, philosophic and economic argument. He
welcomed all to his cause—even the milder slaveholders who accepted the slave system but could not defend it. Douglass argued every question at every level in
his determination to make distinctions and to win the

white mind away from itself. The polemics he employed
were used in turn by his white and black followers all
through the North and in the border states where men
and women felt they could speak out.

The large, bearded figure of Douglass, of the medium-
brown complexion, the mixed lineage—he never knew his
white father—was a stirring presence of the 1840s and
the 1850s.

As the Union stayed together fitfully all through the
1850s, as the great agitation mounted by the Abolitionists and antislavers became more and more a voice in the
nation, and as antislavery criticism influenced the men
in Congress, it could only be a matter of time before
the slave issue itself dominated Congress, America and in
some measure the world. The question was always there,
at varying levels and intensity, popping into sudden
crises like Nullification in 1830, hidden in the inner
meanings of the war against Mexico during the Polk
Administration, influencing Presidential elections from
1830 on.

Now in the 1850s this became the Great Debate of the
Senate and the House of Representatives. There came
violent scenes in the House itself. Senators fought on the
Senate floor hand to hand, hurled canes and inkwells at
each other across the marble halls of freedom. One great
antislavery advocate, Charles Sumner, was hurt so severely that he had to retire from the Senate.

Only *sub rosa* was it felt or stated that the Northern
power structure was, at least in a generalized way, an
antislavery force. It wasn't pro-black, it was only fearful
of the slave power. It wasn't pro-Abolitionist, but it was
for the untrammeled extension of industry westward and
even into the South. It was mostly pro-Caucasian even in
the North right up to the Civil War. But the slave issue
was so much at the heart of the dividing line—and the

slaves were black human beings—that automatically, inevitably, irresistibly, the issue of human rights was there. Neither North nor South could escape this fact.

Sometimes the disputes within the political parties were so rarefied that one would be hard put to realize human beings were involved in the issues, and even at their root. Now and then the issue appeared to be the rich of the North fighting the rich of the South merely over whose riches would survive, and the black man at the core wouldn't even be mentioned in the argument. When they talked of preserving the Union, they really meant the white Union, with or without slaves, with or without Afro-American human beings.

So the power structure developed in the United States. It stood over the black man like an incubus. The incubus sometimes wasn't aware of what moved under it, or of what gave rise to it. But there was the black man, as the core of an apple, full of seeds, and like all seeds full of a potential future.

In the 1850s, the Northerners were rolling up their sleeves; so were the Southerners rolling up theirs. You could see the muscles in every Congressional debate. You could feel the muscles in the demonstrations over fugitive slaves in Boston, New York, Rochester, Cleveland. You could feel the growing tension at times from the silences that occurred.

At the time when the Republican Convention occurred in 1860, in which William H. Seward, who was expected to receive the Republican Presidential nomination was rejected for Lincoln, the Convention itself symbolised a new focus in the national picture. There was now more than a Northern and Southern power structure to contend with; there was a third aspirant to national power, the Frontier, the New West, the people who had moved out beyond the Mississippi to Utah, Oregon, Cal-

ifornia. Those around Indiana, Illinois, Kansas were particularly effectual components of the new force.

Lincoln, a Republican out of Illinois, moved up to
control the party that until then had been led by Eastern
wealth, Eastern statesmen, Eastern politicians. In the
new alignment East and West could unite in a single
political force to counter the weight of the Confederacy.
This was a changed power in the land, a new set of ingredients added to the Northeast wing of national politics. All of this was tacit in the events of the 1850s,
events which would ultimately, through the proslavery
reaction, lead to the firing on Fort Sumter.

Prophecy is an uncertain enterprise. But it has its moments. Washington had predicted an internecine clash
over slavery; Jefferson intimated that by one means or
another, even by mystic, supernatural means, it was possible for the slave to rise out of his bonds.

And now it was being done. Forces larger than men
were bringing about a collision which would produce
cataclysmic consequences. But this impending clash
raised many questions. To what extent were the forces
economic? How much of this was simple conflict for
profit between Northern industry and Southern slavery?
How much moral force was there on the side of the industrial legions? How deep was the involvement of the
religious, moral, philosophic and intellectual protest currents of the day in the cause of human freedom? How
much of this moralist base was entailed in the formation
of the abstract force of Northern-Republican political
power that was now moving into Washington? And how
much was the human equation, the drive of men who in
spite of all else insist on being or becoming free?

We know now that a world of factors and forces had
brought slavery this far, from 1430 through 1850. Men,
women, Bibles, churches, books, guns, philosophies, pol-

icies, laws had combined to make the two divisions of American power, and now all these influences were in transmogrification. Real and mystic alterations of great force were there, as armies prepared to meet on battle-fields.

Could the war have been averted? Seward and others wanted to avert the war by having Lincoln declare war on France, England, Russia, virtually the whole world, so as to compel the North and the South to stay united and to confront a common enemy elsewhere, and not fight among themselves.

But by now events too enormous, too economic, too variegated were in propulsion. Lincoln told Seward that he was committed by the nomination to prevent the spread of slavery into the West; this was one thing that had to be settled first. He didn't accept the foreign war approach; his own feeling was that the North would have to defend itself against the developing Confederate secession.

In the backdrops the restive and essentially rebellious slaves worked on. They remained in the fields. They fed Southern armies and Southern civilians, unable to do otherwise. Aware that the North was going to war against their oppressors in the South, still the slaves were so rived, so patrolled, so held to the Southern tradition, that they remained shackled to the plantations which fed the men and the armies that were pledged to keep them forever in chains. Such was the anomaly. Such was the depressed character of the American Negro, the mass of the slaves, as the war opened.

The nation now had a population of about thirty millions. Ten millions were located in the South, and one-third of that population was slave. Outnumbering of the black by only two to one was not too great an advantage.

All through the 1850s the slaves engaged in outbreaks, some fair-sized local revolts. Individual tyrannical slave-owners were slain; the Negroes fled North if they could. It was this rising spirit of unrest in the South that gave John Brown the idea that if he launched a revolution in Virginia, slaves might come to his assistance.

There was also a large non-slaveowning South of poor whites, farmers, laborers and unemployed who had no profound sympathy for the slavemasters, their wealth, their arrogance nor their pretensions. This wing of moneyless and indebted whites could see as well as any-one else that the system under which they lived lagged behind the promise of the developments in the North. Thousands in the South knew that urbanization of the North and the spread of manufacturing combined to make the free labor wage system a more operable and effective force for the changing times.

In the South itself, rich and poor were at odds. A few thousand slaveholders owned most of the slaves; most of the other 300,000 slaveowners owned only one, two, or rarely, as many as half a dozen. The most powerful plan-tation owners earned the enmity of the less opulent.

In 1854, about 430,000 immigrants moved into the United States. A majority headed for farms in the West, but many stayed in the growing cities. Within a few years New York reached the million-population mark. The new arrivals liked the size of the city, the bustle, the big buildings, the opportunities to make money. The new-comers provided new markets for the North, and in con-sequence greater industrial activity; they had to be fed, moved, housed, clothed. The West began shipping goods back East and the East shipped it abroad or consumed it. The North was beginning to revolve around a railroad economy. Before the war broke out railroads accounted for a billion and a half dollars of investment, a capitalization level with which the South could no longer compete. Manufacture of agricultural machinery became a basic industry of the Middle West. American threshing machines outsped those made in any other country; by the time John Brown marched on Harper's Ferry, northern invention and science and mechanics led the world.

In the South many plantation owners with used-up fields of soil were forced to move into the Southwest to find new land where their kind of cotton and tobacco production could go on. They watched how industry in the North was placing a sewing machine in every house, how cheap steel was being made by something new called the Bessemer process, invented in 1847. These were some of the forces that made the Southern crisis and activated Southerners in their frantic efforts to get more and more blacks to man more and more farm fields.

The North was already old enough to have slums in some of its big cities, but that often provided a pretext for new housing. In the South the big old colonial mansions became mouldier and new wings were added: while the blacks lived in large groups in simple board shacks.

The contrasts of living standards became sharper. There were two different worlds, two different nations, two different ways of thinking.

Those with little stake in slave property were trying to organize politically and they were advancing and uniting at the time of the schismatic political changes of 1859 and 1860. The slavocracy was afraid of pressures from below. Poor white and slave Negro could even unite against them. In the North a large antislavery movement did unite Negro and white. If it happened in the North it could someday happen below the line. Informed Southern leaders knew that thirty or forty years earlier most of the antislavery societies were in the South.

Their whole situation was untenable.

Economic experts among the slave holding forces worried about a fundamental change taking place in the nation's economy. Until the 1850s agricultural production dominated, and with this went almost automatically political domination of the nation by the slave power, the prime agricultural producer. In the 1850s, industrial production equalled the agricultural. That was when the tide began turning toward the Northern economy. That was when both North and South looked westward to see who would control federal land and which social system would conquer the West. The North had the advantage. Where the slave system needed always more slaves and more land to produce more cotton, Northern mechanization could achieve greater production in smaller quarters with fewer people. Factories now had well-organized assembly lines. The new era of mass production techniques had begun.

Added to the South's need for expansion and the North's capacity for concentration was the continual shifting pattern of population migrations. Annually there was an influx from Europe of several hundred thousand new working people. They stopped first in the North usually, often in the cities, then moved westward toward the Mississippi. They did not produce or depend upon cotton, tobacco, sugar or rice. They cultivated corn, wheat and rye; they went into cattle and sheep raising; they dealt in leather, furniture, lumbering, and countless other occupations, giving variety to their economy. They were not dependent upon one or two crops and slaves to produce them as were the Southerners. Some of these immigrants, the Germans, brought with them a tradition of liberalism, labor and trade unionism and planted these ideas wherever they went. This actually strengthened and advanced free labor and business in the North.

Slaveholders feared Eastern wealth and the way in which the East, through building railroads, sought trade with the farmers from Ohio to Mississippi. In despair they saw the railroads building a network across the North and into the West and they could see the railroad clique itself as a major economic group inside the Northern structure. Some Southerners hoped they could work out an alliance between slavery and the farming population of the West. This led to the sharp struggle over Kansas, but the decisive elements here were the immigrant farmers who leaned to mechanization, free labor, mineral exploitation and industrial advance.

Desperation, panic, fear of bankruptcy, internal troubles throughout the South and a futile competition with the new social system that was sweeping the North and had been changing much of Europe for several centuries —these forces drove the slaveholding people to speak of secession and seek support for that idea among all Southern whites.

They did not want a test of the question by ballot. A poll on breaking with the Union might be defeated. Southern leaders knew they were split down the middle. Their leaders weren't certain of the support of the non-slaveholding majority if they pulled away from the Union. Before secession occurred, one state, Texas, took a poll and more than a hundred thousand voted to secede while nearly fifty thousand were opposed. In two other states, Virginia and Tennessee, the issue was placed before the electorate after secession took place and the vote emerged about fifty-fifty for and against secession. In eight other states the slave forces would not submit the matter to a vote. Such a split and such an undemocratic procedure in the eight states reveal how desperate the slave power was and how fearful it was of dissent in its own provinces.

Besides this anti-secessionist sentiment there were a half dozen border states, each with large slave populations, with racialist attitudes as prevalent as in those farther South; but even the border states wanted to remain aloof from a seceding Confederacy.

The pattern is seen in what happened after the newly-elected Lincoln ordered 75,000 troops to be mobilised. Four of the middle-country states, Missouri, Kentucky, Delaware and Maryland, decided to stay neutral. This was a meaningful force in terms of population, territory, location. There were slaves and free Negroes in these states. Maryland had a tradition in Southern ways about as old as Virginia's. That these states, aged in the same agricultural tradition as those which had seceded, could decide to avoid being swept by the hysteria of the Confederacy, is another confirmation of the depth of the South's internal differences.

As so often happens, the Southern power structure saddled an unwilling people with an unpopular war. *The secession was from the top.*

The War with Mexico a few years earlier had been put over on the people in the same way, with the frontier-pushing Southern States instigating it and going ahead with it because the slavocracy was in federal power. The South was close to Mexico, it had military means, it needed land, and it simply ignored Northern and Southern sentiment against Mexican invasion. That military event had ended as recently as 1848, and the secessionists with military experience remembered how they had promoted that invasion, independent of sentiment anywhere in the North or the South; this recollection helped to stimulate the Southerners into feeling they could be militarily successful again if they continued to go over the head of public sentiment. Again, working from the top, the officialdom of a half dozen Southern States organized a Confederate Constitutional Convention. They then set up a Confederate States of America, elected Jefferson Davis as provisional president, and steamrollered a largely unwilling South into civil war.

The man who fired the first shot against Fort Sumter was a well-to-do slaveowner named Edmund Ruffin, a powerful advocate of secession. Like so many on official levels he kept a diary. In his private records he recorded that delegates to the Confederate Constitutional Convention held in February, 1861, after six states seceded, knew they were engaged upon an unpopular course. The delegates let one another know that a majority of the people in each Southern state except South Carolina were against the disruption of the nation. Ruffin noted that some delegates surmised that if the matter of returning to the Union was put to a Southwide vote then and there, in 1861, the people would probably approve of reconstructing the states as a united nation.

In short, the South wasn't solid at all. It was split up and fell prey to the divide-and-panic tactics of the secession organizers who undertook to corral, conscript and dragoon as many as they could, mercilessly in whatever way they could, to wage war against the Union. But such measures and such unsettled attitudes contained the seeds of demoralization that would haunt the empty homes of the Confederates within a few years. Dragooning hundreds of thousands of men into a war to preserve an obsolete social form did not encourage ultimate morale or fervor that would make for final military success. And, hardly considered in the background, the heaving black population didn't intend making it any easier for the masters and the racists they despised.

A final measure of the size of this split force was

affirmed in the national elections of 1860, just before actual war began. Two Democratic parties entered the field, a Northern and a Southern. But when the votes were counted there was far from any pro-slavery unity even among the Southern Democrats. Breckinridge of Kentucky, a secessionist, the Southern Democrat candidate for President, found that more Southerners voted against him than for him. The split between the two Democratic parties led to the election of Lincoln; but the voting revealed the disparities of viewpoint in the South.

Every time the fissures opened wider and the slaveholders beheld how broad and numerous the fissures were, they intensified their secessionist sentiment. By the time Lincoln was elected, they knew the South was going to pull out, to make a stab at independent survival as a nation at no matter what price.

Willian H. Seward may have been right when he said that no civil war was necessary and that the slave power would bankrupt and crumble from within or with but little pressure at some point in the future. But those in danger of losing power would rather fight than yield. And that was the road the Confederacy chose.

At the time of the Battle of Manassas, Negroes of the North and slaves of the South looked at one another with wondering eyes. Southern master was fighting Northern master; white folks were divided and killing each other. The slaves looked upon the Northern officialdom as an uncertain semi-enemy. They knew that the North often returned fugitive slaves, that free Negroes above the Mason-Dixon line were only quasi-free, that the vituperation of Northern officials, leaders, churchmen, spokesmen often equalled that of the Southerners. To the slave, there was a large degree of blood-kin unity between white ruler up North and white master below. Still, the

two were now at war. Where would it lead? What did Mr.
Lincoln intend to do with the Southern Negroes?

Events were confirming a prediction made by James
Madison long before, that a crisis might conceivably lift
this dehumanised portion of society out of its condition if
the right circumstances occurred. Here now were the
right circumstances. The Negro as a "party" was ready to
identify himself with the Northern-Republican-Union
force, and the latter needed the black. Out of this lever-
age might come that re-humanising prospect Madison
suggested.

From the earliest days of the war, Union successes in
Confederate territory freed groups of Negroes. Two
Union generals issued emancipation orders in local areas
to demoralise the Confederacy and to waken all possible
slave support. Major General John Fremont in March,
1862, freed slaves seized from Missouri secessionists.
Lincoln, cautious about inciting the Confederacy, re-
scinded the order. The same thing occurred the next
month at Hilton Head, South Carolina, when Major
General David Hunter decreed slaves free in the Department of the South. Lincoln was angered and again nulli-
fied the order, once more motivated by a desire not to
antagonise the Confederacy, or to risk losing the neutrality of the border states. Perhaps he was not even certain
at that time that he wanted Negroes freed at all inside the
American context; it is known that for some time he
devoutly favored their removal to Panama, to the West
Indies or to Africa.

In addition to those slaves liberated by local military
actions, others, sensing that the Union cause was theirs,
escaped to Union encampments. Known as "contraband," these were the first human harbingers of the developing problem of reconstruction. Many were placed
in "contraband camps" where the living was poor; and
disease carried away a percentage of them.

The paucity of Federal policy on freeing slaves, the enormity of the crisis which stretched over several thousand miles of terrain and involved thirty millions of people, the precipitate character of the secession, the rather automatic marshalling of the Northern force and the steady drift into more extensive warfare all combined to make the slave's future unclear. In the first year and a quarter of the warfare it wasn't official that the slave was even a vital issue in the context of the war.

For the time being approximately four million slaves were trapped as the supply force of Southern arms—in Southern factories and fields.

Studying how the secessionists were using the slave to grow food and do the heavy labor job required to keep the South going, Lincoln gave thought on how to turn the slave supply to the Union cause. To announce them free roused in him fears of a vindictive Confederate retaliation and fears that even some of the Northern officers and privates would not fight or might lay down their arms; moreover, the possibility that neutral border states might bolt to the Southern cause was a constant nightmare. Retaining the neutrality of states which appeared to hold the balance of power became a one-man diplomatic operation of his own. His hesitations as he viewed these states caused him to defer issuing an Emancipation Proclamation. Keeping these states out of the fighting was the equivalent of neutralizing several enemy divisions. With the passage of time Lincoln began to think about "military necessity," the same term which Washington ultimately used to justify his policy of enlisting Negroes in the colonial cause to prevent them from going over to the British.

The decisive battle of the Civil War from a military standpoint was Gettysburg; but the other big battle, the one in Lincoln's mind for fifteen months before he issued the Emancipation Proclamation, may have been as decisive.

Freedom and slavery ticked inside the President like a pendulum in a clock. Abstractly he was for black deliverance from chattel slavery; but realistically he was, like the overwhelming majority of Caucasians, not quite able to act in accordance with his abstract emotions. About the only future he saw for slaves was colonization away from United States soil. Yet he expressed his uncertainties once when he said, "If we could first know where we are and whither we are tending, we could better judge what to do and how to do it."

The war became defined in Lincoln's mind, as well as in the mind of the public North and South, as a contest involving two principles: dominion over the American continent and the perseveration or ending of chattel slavery. When Lincoln talked of Union, he meant the dominion struggle. Which system would dominate after the war? Which would organize, control and fill up the West? He tried to keep the purpose of the war upon that level as long as he could. But the root question of human slavery kept seeping to the surface like black oil. The issue was human freedom or human bondage—this before all else.

How to keep the Union together was largely military at the outset. But neither Lincoln nor anyone else had clearly thought out what to do about the Afro-American's future, and even the white American's future. The questions were fraught with sectional, racial, caste, business and labor issues. Morality, justice, human decency and human depravity were all involved in the contest with slavery. Here were two contraposed social systems:

in one you pay wages, in the other you do not; in one a man is a soul and a body, in the other the soul and body belongs to another man. Unless provision were made for changes such as work projects, or a system of employment in private industry, or the granting of land to slaves, or introduction of a wage-labor economy into the South, or migration northward of freed men into non-slavery labor, great confusion was certain to develop.

Lincoln was a Southerner. He was born in Kentucky and he lived there until the age of eight. What he saw or knew of black folk we cannot be too sure of now. You can find both sides of his views on slavery in his writings. You can find quotations as early as 1837, when he was a freshman in Congress, saying that slavery was founded upon injustice and bad policy. Later when he was progressing politically and had to consider Southern policy, votes and slave owner pressure, he said that there were sharp physical differences between black and white and if there was any question about which one was to be superior he was in favor of the white remaining superior. Like his great predecessor, George Washington, he would get on the trapeze and swing back over into the realm of conscience and the prickings thereof. If slavery isn't wrong, he said, then nothing is wrong. But there was inconsistency. He was nagged by the feeling of a deep racial gulf: to him it was physiological-biological. There is no other word to describe it but racial, for Lincoln's most cherished belief *á propos* solutions to the slave problems was the same as Jefferson's: we cannot live with them, so colonise them. This colonising outlook was close to his heart well into the waging of the Civil War. At last he found himself almost alone with this conviction and unable to implement it.

Lincoln, a lawyer and a Constitutionalist, regarded his Presidential position as largely a legalistic, an official role. He didn't want to free the Negroes if it might be unconstitutional. He respected states rights, and since the purpose of the war was to hold the Union together and restore amity between the states, the idea, he thought, was to respect legality and code as much as possible. If slaves had to be emancipated, he believed the nation had to pay the slaveholders. Give the masters every inducement to feel that they were part of the Union. Late in 1861 he worked on a project of paying willing states for the gradual emancipation of slaves. The states would be paid so much per head. Only a half day's cost of the war would pay for all the slaves in Delaware at four hundred dollars apiece, Lincoln pointed out. The cost of eighty-seven days of the war would pay for the freeing of all the slaves in Maryland, Delaware, Kentucky, Missouri and the District of Columbia. Congress actually passed such a resolution early in 1862. But the states rejected it. What was four hundred dollars for a slave against the income from using a slave for life?

In the South, several million human beings (even if they weren't yet regarded as such) continued to work for the Confederacy by force. Their will had not yet been brought into the picture on the side of the Union. Soon after the war opened, in May of 1861, Frederick Douglass campaigned for that black will to be entered upon the side of the Union. In speeches and writings he implied that every kind of economic and legal consideration appeared in the White House vacillation, but there was little evidence yet of a true antislavery attitude.

In an article published in May of 1861, Douglass depicted how the war might be won. He called for the use of free Negroes to march into the South and to raise the banner of emancipation among the slaves. A full year later Douglass found himself still arguing the same point, saying that slavery was at the root of this war and the issue shouldn't be limited to Union preservation at the slave's cost. Thus legalisms, moral vacillations and military expediency, had dominated the thinking of the man from Illinois at that time.

At the outset of hostilities, Charles Sumner, ranking Republican spokesman in the Senate, told Lincoln that it might be all right to talk about Union preservation then, but a little later emancipation must become the policy. Sumner continued his pressure, but Lincoln wouldn't rush matters. He might never free the slave, he said. If that would keep the Union together, then so be it.

Week after week Lincoln resisted friends, delegations, meetings which pressed upon him the urgency of freeing the chattels. He turned down Quakers in the summer of 1862, saying to them that a decree alone wouldn't free any slaves. Close to Lincoln was a cautious Seward who didn't think highly of an emancipation document if the Union couldn't back it up militarily. Presbyterians went to see Lincoln, urging immediate emancipation. But he told them that what they asked of him was surgery, and sometimes in surgery a man could bleed to death. He wouldn't be pushed.

Horace Greeley reached the President in August of 1862 with an eloquent editorial in *The Tribune* bearing the title, "The Prayer of Twenty Millions." Greeley intimated that Lincoln was himself flouting the law by not freeing the slaves, for the President had rebellion on his hands and he ought to act against it. Lincoln was touched by this, as he was touched by all appeals. But the Chief told Greeley that he would do anything to save the Union even if it meant not freeing a single slave.

Lincoln's policy on Union preservation was much clearer than his policy on Negroes as slaves, as men, or as figures with potential American rights. On September 13th, 1862, Lincoln met with a Christian delegation from Chicago, but this time it was ecumenical and religionists of all creeds who were urging him to act. Lincoln told them that proslavery religionists who also believed in Christ and in God had, with the same vehemence, urged him not to emancipate the Negroes.

The heart of Lincoln's problem—and the nation's—appeared when he told the ministers from Chicago that he didn't know what to do with the slaves if he did free them.

It was in that kernel statement that the whole future of Reconstruction, with all that was to happen between 1865 through 1877, was contained. How could the Union feed four million emancipated blacks? What would *you* do with them? How would you reconstruct them inside the system that Northerners lived by and believed in? His questions went unanswered.

Therein was the seed. Lincoln had no program for taking care of freed slaves. Nobody else did. The military exigencies, the danger of defeat by the Confederacy, apparently forestalled serious thinking about any postwar program. The petitioners simply wanted a decree—which they were to get. It would lend morale to the Union cause, give point to the war. But because nobody looked into the future to "win the peace," or visualise the care or reemployment of so many millions who must be lifted from so low a situation, out of these variables, would come the confused, crippled era of Reconstruction.

Aware that there was no program for handling the Negroes after their deliverance, Lincoln once asked Frederick Douglass who would take care of them and what should be done with them. The colored leader answered that they should be allowed to take care of themselves, as others did. Anxious for the big change, willing to take one step at a time, Douglass told the President that if the blacks could take care of their masters they could take care of themselves.

If one system of labor relations was crushed out of history and no new operable plan of labor relations was put forward in its stead, only complication could result. Yet nothing in the American experience enabled Lincoln and his advisers to determine how and what to do with such a huge mass of delivered people. Nobody suggested apportioning land to the Negroes, although the nation had land to spare.

Lincoln possessed enough of the racial vein to say to a group of Negroes late in 1862, "You and we are different races. Whether it is right or wrong I need not discuss. But this physical difference is a great disadvantage to us both, as I think your race suffer very greatly, many of them by living among us, while ours suffer from your presence. In a word we suffer on each side. If this be admitted, it affords a reason why at least we should be separated." He then proposed colonization away from the United States. That was the only postwar solution that appeared clear to him. Few antislavers liked the idea and Negroes rejected it wholly.

When it came to colonization Lincoln could visualise money available, ships ready to carry the Negroes away, purchase of territory in Africa or somewhere else. All the details were clear.

As far back as 1854 he remarked that his own impulse would be to free the slaves and to send them back to Liberia, to their native land. He talked colonization in his first annual message, and in April of 1862 he favored colonization of Negro freedmen in the District of Columbia. Two months later he directed legislation to appropriate a half million dollars to ship them out. He sent a special message to Congress asking for action to finance such a project. Secretary of State Seward began correspondence with Great Britain, France, Sweden, Denmark, and the South American countries to see who would take black refugees. Only the island of Vache, which was part of Haiti, replied favorably. It never worked out.

The idea of colonization was central to the preliminary Emancipation Proclamation which Lincoln began preparing in the spring or early summer of 1862. The President went about this in a very private way for some time. Delegations still harrassed him about the need for a liberation policy and they did not know he was working upon a plan with that effect in mind. Military events had gone from bad to worse, Lincoln said later; he felt that the Union cause had reached the end of its rope with the plan of operations that had been pursued and the tactics must be changed or the game would be lost. It was then that he determined on the adoption of the emancipation policy "Without consultation with, or knowledge of the Cabinet, I prepared the original draft of the proclamation . . ."

During the summer months he took into his confidence one person after another, disclosing that he was formulating an important document. A telegraph operator, Thomas Eckert, in the telegraph room of the War Department, where Lincoln liked to work in privacy, may have been the first to know what Lincoln was doing. Later the Chief Executive told Secretary of War Stanton about what pressed upon his mind; and he promised Senator Charles Sumner that within a couple of months an emancipation decree would go out to the world. Vice President Hannibal Hamlin had also urged Lincoln to issue a proclamation and one day in the middle of June Lincoln told Hamlin that he intended heeding the Vice President's advice and similar counsel of others; then he opened his desk drawer and removed a draft of the document. Hamlin read it and judged that the proclamation was exclusively Lincoln's, with Lincoln's ideas well spelled out, including colonization.

When Union armies met with serious defeat at Richmond—about fifteen months after Lincoln took office—he became more convinced than ever before that he had to make the proclamation.

On Sunday, July 13th, 1862, he was a figure in an early morning funeral procession that moved through the streets of Washington to a cemetery on the outskirts of the capital. A dozen coaches containing members of the Cabinet and their families were accompanying Secretary of War Stanton to the cemetery for the burial of his infant son. A white coach carrying the small white casket of the infant went first. Behind, in Stanton's coach, Lincoln sat at the War Secretary's side and opposite sat Secretary of State William Henry Seward and Secretary of the Navy Gideon Welles. After a time of quiet Lincoln's words broke the hush: "If the rebels do not soon cease their war on the Goverment and the Union. I believe we shall have to do something essential that I have been thinking about for some time."

He went on, "I am thinking it may be necessary to emancipate the slaves by proclamation. I see no evidence that the rebels will cease to persist in their war on the Government. I know that what I speak of is a grave step, but I have given it much thought no matter how delicate the matter, and I have reached the conclusion that this is now a military necessity absolutely essential for the salvation of the Union."

Lincoln's words pictured the pressures of the time, the issues involved, and the crisis of the war itself which appeared to make an Emancipation Proclamation necessary. It seemed to him that they must either free the slaves or themselves be subdued. He saw no other solution. Seward agreed; he thought the Cabinet ought to consider the step seriously. Welles agreed with Seward. No one disagreed with Lincoln; the only issue was when to time such an announcement.

Less than ten weeks later, after the battle of Antietam, the timing seemed right, and on September 22nd, Lincoln issued a preliminary Emancipation Proclamation. The document stated that on January 1st, 1863, in all those states which were then still in rebellion, the slaves would go free.

The first paragraph of the Proclamation declared that the war would continue to be prosecuted for the object of restoring the constitutional relation between the states. The next paragraph promised a Congressional recommendation of compensated emancipation for states not in rebellion who would adopt plans for immediate or gradual emancipation of their slaves, adding, "and that the effort to colonize persons of African descent, with their consent, upon this continent, or elsewhere, with the previously obtained consent of the Governments existing there, will be continued."

Colonization clearly remained Lincoln's main idea of the slave's liberation.

That Lincoln could go this far, offering even a compromise Proclamation, may have been, in the exigencies of that hour, remarkable. After the routine hailings of the Act from more or less expected circles, opposition to the decree began making its appearance. It came from Northern Democrats, from an outraged Democratic South, and from Republican Party figures who feared that the action would lead to political defeat for their party at the Fall, 1862, elections. Western Republicans in particular expected the Proclamation to lose their states to the Democrats.

The fears and predictions were borne out in October as Democrats swept into office in Pennsylvania, Indiana and Ohio. The next month Democrats won in New York, New Jersey, Delaware and Illinois.

Reverses for the Republicans indicated a distinct limit to public thinking in the North and West about freeing slaves. Millions still believed the only valid or worthwhile issue was to hold the Union together.

These soft underbelly portions of the North and West were to stay soft and proslavery through the Reconstruction time; they would constitute the force which from 1865 through 1877 urged and worked for abandonment of the black man to the mercies of his former owners.

During the hundred days that elapsed from the time of the issuance of the preliminary Proclamation through to the announcement of the final one, Lincoln was placed in a position where he had to stiffen his purposes. He must either respond to that pressure which opposed emancipation on January 1st, or liberate with an extra sharpness and definitiveness. He chose the latter course.

When the revised Proclamation was released on January 1st, it omitted colonization from its contents. It threw all emphasis upon the entry of the slave into the prevailing Union-Northern economy; and it added force to the military opportunity to the Negroes to join up with the Union.

The President realized that it was contradictory to free the slaves, to expect to use them in the Union military engagements, and then ship them off to Africa or Central America. The colonization policy, intended to appeal to racialist thinking in border states, in the Confederacy and even to Northern anti-Negro feelings, was totally abandoned.

The silence on colonization and the new approach meant that the fate of black and white must be worked out upon American soil.

The final Emancipation Proclamation varied profoundly from the preliminary document. In the sixth paragraph it stated that "all persons held as slaves within said designated States (the ones in rebellion) are, and henceforward shall be free; and that the Executive government of the United States, including the military and naval authority thereof, will recognize and maintain freedom of said persons."

This meant that the freedmen would fall immediately under Union military aegis and so be enabled to receive the protection of the Union Army as a free labor force for the first time.

The next paragraph implied the right of the freedmen to take up arms in the Union behalf. "And I hereby enjoin upon the people so declared to be free to abstain from all violence, unless in necessary self-defence . . ." Yet for all practical purposes that meant, "Join the Union Army and fight, for you will have to defend yourselves if you are to go free and to stay free."

The next clause referred to the slave's break with his past and indicated where he would go thereafter: ". . . and I recommend to them that, in all cases when allowed, they labor faithfully for reasonable wages."

This was much different from Lincoln's earlier plan of colonization. In three months he had taken an enormous step forward in his thinking and acting. Now he faced full-on the truth that slaves must and would go on living in the United States. Henceforward the new citizens would enter upon the free enterprise economy alongside their white brothers.

In Lincoln's case it can be said that whatever ambivalence he had, whatever his duality about white-Negro values, lost significance in the power with which he finally moved. The act of emancipation was so overwhelming as to swamp whatever reservations he had and whatever have been attributed to him. Military necessity swept away all temporizing. The first grand act of integration upon our soil, outweighed and undid the racialism that had lingered in him from childhood.

By and large the Proclamation was hailed here and abroad, and years later in retrospect, as one of the handful of great official documents of the modern era.

In the South it excited a reaction of horror. To the Confederacy it was a case of civilized men in the North aiding insurrection. It seemed to Secessionist officialdom a great violation of the faith that ought to exist between leading classes, between peoples of the same blood.

Jefferson Davis, addressing the Confederate Congress two weeks after the Proclamation appeared, said: "We may well leave it to the instincts of that common humanity which a beneficent Creator has implanted in the breasts of our fellow-men of all countries to pass judgment on a measure by which several millions of human beings of an inferior race, peaceful and contented laborers in their spheres, are doomed to extermination, while at the same time they are encouraged to a general assassination of their masters by the insidious recommendation to 'abstain from violence unless in necessary self-defense.' "

It became clear that the Civil War itself was only one battle in the long historical development of black liberation and United States evolution. The whole succeeding century was to become a battlefield only less violent than that of the period 1861 through 1865.

The Proclamation changed the course of the war. It gave to the conflict that resolve and purpose which had so far been lacking.

Jubilation became translated at once into a variety of experiences for the Negro population. Thousands of Negroes went to Union lines or headed North and the Confederacy could not halt the exodus. Four million colored non-combatants in the service of the Confederacy now became an unreliable labor force. Sabotage of the Confederate cause intensified; black men by the thousands swept into the armed forces of the Union. During the Spring of 1863 twenty regiments of Negroes in states which had come under Union aegis joined up. By the end of the war about 190,000 black troops were engaged with the Union Armies. The blue-uniformed Negroes, about ten percent of the total Union force, took part in forty major engagements and participated in a total of five hundred military operations.

One-third of the black fighting forces was killed in action.

The war brought into the foreground all the ramifications of black-white association. Colored and white often fought side by side. One Negro woman, Harriet Tubman, led white and black troops on the field of battle in at least one engagement. A regiment of Afro-Americans, the 54th, was annihilated in an especially important engagement at Fort Wagner. Black soldiers often rose in rank and at least one, a Pittsburgh man named Martin Delany, became a major. Whites North and South learned that the black could fight well for his own freedom if given a chance to handle arms.

While white soldiers fought side by side with the black in many engagements, there were many battles in which only Negro troops met the Confederate soldiers. Moreover, Confederate wrath against black troops was especially severe.

As the striking power of the Confederacy became reduced and as the Northern army, enlarged by colored soldiers, increased in morale, organization and punch, changes in the war began appearing which would not be clearly perceived until later, when the conflict ended and the impact of the Proclamation could be measured. Lincoln lived to see how the Proclamation, firing Negro morale, was followed by the strengthening of the Union's military situation. Near the end of the war's course he remarked on several occasions that the accession of the black fighting force was significant in the Union victory.

Abolitionists, Negro leaders and radical Republicans pressed for a Constitutional Amendment to prohibit slavery throughout the nation. Lincoln knew that he had to go beyond the limitations of the Proclamation. After he was re-elected in 1864 he moved rapidly in the direction of making that amendment a reality, and on January 31st, 1865, the House voted the amendment doing away with slavery, an action hailed as the greatest step ever taken by Congress.

THROUGH RECONSTRUCTION

In the first practical stroke of Government, when Lincoln proposed that Negro soldiers be given half-pay, there began the halfway-secondclass citizenship status which was to endure. Lincoln believed that the country should become accustomed to the idea of Negroes soldiering before they received full pay and promotions. Later they did secure full pay, but the compromise had re-entered, just as it had entered the Constitution.

Perhaps little in the history of the Western Hemisphere, its revolts and emancipations in other countries, as in South America or in the West Indies, contained "lessons" applicable to the American scene and needs immediately after the Civil War. No serious study was made of great changes in European history or in any other history; few if any proposals were based upon experiences anywhere else in the world.

Lincoln had touched the core of it all when he asked the religionist delegation: How can the Union feed and care for them? Nobody looked ahead to that day when the slave would have to be ready for freedom. Nobody had a plan, a chart, a proposal about funds or lands or work for the newly emancipated black man. Nobody came to Lincoln and said: "Here is what we do with four million newly-liberated slaves."

As a result of the way in which the fateful collision of war had occurred, with the South precipitately seceding, with battles, including Gettysburg, unplanned at the outset, with Lincoln maintaining that holding the Union together was the central objective, not black freedom, there was laid a groundwork for the confusions which followed the end of war.

The break from chattel slavery was clear—but that was all. Nothing else was solid, clear, or established. The black man, and millions of poor whites, in a manner of speaking, went on relief. They went into camps; they were cared for as refugees, as "problems," not as new citizens of a new promised land.

They entered into a limbo, without finances, food or work, often even without huts to sleep in. They became dependent upon the Union Army, Abolitionist officers and antislavery soldiers. Their experience was an expulsion from slavery rather than any admittance to a civilization.

Finally with the assassination, Lincoln's program of gradual liberation, never clearly outlined, was cut off before it really began, and conditions for the bumbling, warring excesses of Reconstruction were at hand.

The South, bold and militant in its rebellion, held to its racist character even after defeat on the field of battle, and there was a natural extension of this attitude into Reconstruction.

With the programmatic features of the post-war period vague or unplanned, with the North dedicated more or less to a pragmatic, day-by-day handling of events, much of the groundwork for Reconstruction confusion was established. The rest occurred when the South, taking advantage of the assassination, the paralysis of the country, the panic of the Northern parties, and the accession to the Presidency of its devout partisan, Andrew Johnson, moved to reconsolidate.

Half-way and even full-way measures were from now on met by massive counter-revolutionary strength of an embittered Confederacy intending with all its manpower and twisted spiritual energy to find means to keep Afro-Americans from sharing full and equal rule.

There began at once, but at a different level and with new half-working mechanisms, a nationwide recreation of the role, status and categorization of the colored population. No one could see at the outset that what was in the making was not full liberation but caste. A new churning process began somewhat similar to the original man-making at the Factories on the Gold Coast centuries earlier. All the phenomena were present in the post-Emancipation period which would slightly elevate yet still obscure and blur the black man's status. The chattel relationship was broken, but the Democratic South, moving instantly into action, began to restore itself to full power and to recapture control of the Negro along new lines.

Lifted from slavery, placed in the benevolent hands of antislavery Northerners and a partially dedicated federal government, but still under the aegis of an unreconstructed slavocracy, the Afro-American was caught in a vise of peoples, sections, economies, parties and conflicting theories. He was immediately beset by limitations written and unwritten. He was not permitted to work at wages in any practical way either in the North or the South. Disruption was great in the South. The new economy was jagged, wages were unregulated, Southern businessmen did not even have the means to pay wages; yet most Negroes were destined to stay in the South. An economy of poverty set in, involving masses of white and black, and fixing the Southern economy so that it lagged behind the Northern undisrupted system. The black people had no land, no money, no real jobs. They remained partly-liberated slaves.

There was an entire West that remained still untapped and the struggle for that West was a large part of the reason for the conflict between North and South, but none of this West was available to any segment of Negroes who might wish to settle and cultivate and own land. The West was freed mainly for railroad and mineral conquest by the white North and for its settlement primarily by new hundreds of thousands of Europeans who flooded the region during the next two or three decades. The Negroes actually dreamed of owning land— anywhere. They talked and dreamed of forty acres and a mule—but how could they extricate themselves from the poverty-ridden stranglehold of plantation life?

Emancipation did not signify social equality with whites North or South. Such equality was found only on local levels among Abolitionists and white men and women of unusual good will. Even so, social communication between black and white was more extensive in Reconstruction than at any time before, equalled only by fraternal relationships in today's civil rights movement.

At once there began a piecemeal fight, in which both North and South participated, over what the colored person was and was not entitled to. Was he entitled to the same education as a white Northern child, or a white Southern child? Should he be allowed to vote, to function as a juryman, to bring suit? Did he have the right to bear arms in his own defense? Should Negro births be recorded? Was it desirable for black men and women legally to marry? Should they be allowed marriage licenses or should they be forced to cohabit without legal privilege? Every bit of legal extension was contested by someone somewhere, by some officialdom locally or upon a state level.

If the man-making nature of our society were legally brought to an end during the war, if a de-inventive process were written into the Constitution—and it was so written—still the countervailing force of the Confederacy, plus the subsequent indifference of much of the official North, was to hamstring and distort that liberation.

What resulted during the next fifty years was the creation of two new kinds of Americans: millions of prejudiced white folks with distorted views, and polar to these, a mass of alienated, restricted, semi-freed Afro-Americans.

The death of the President was followed by unparalleled political crisis, some of which stemmed from the assassination, the rest from the disunion that remained after the surrender of Lee at Appomattox. The most complicated feature was that Congress was not in session and it would not reconvene until eight months after the President's death. In this two-thirds of a year the North, through the Radical Republicans, girded to reconstruct the South. The Confederacy, taking advantage of the time element, the national paralysis and the general crisis, moved at once to restore to itself its old image of power.

That interim, with no federally sponsored program, no Republican Party unity, with Democrats North and South plotting for recovery of control, may have been as decisive for the history of the nation as Gettysburg. Only this was no victory, but a period of reversal for the Union cause.

The strong probability is that with Lincoln's humanity, and even with his programmatic uncertainty about how to reconstitute blacks inside the national life, Negro progress would have been more assured, their evolution into the national life quicker, had he remained alive during the crucial second administration. Though feared and opposed by "full equality Republicans" as too moderate and conservative, Lincoln's middle-of-the-road handling might have produced better results than what happened as a result of the tug of war that developed between the Radicals and the violent-minded reborn Democratic night riders.

Radical Republicans, waiting for Congress to reconvene, sought to visualize the size of their objectives for the coming years. Their position was best expressed by Senator Thaddeus Stevens who wanted the complete equality implied by the Emancipation Proclamation and

the new amendments to the Constitution. He conceived
that the line in the Declaration of Independence that "all
men are created equal" was an Americanism that meant
what it said. The whole fabric of Southern society must
be changed, he argued, even if this drove the South's so-
called nobility into exile.

Senator Charles Sumner, leader of the House Republicans, believed that if all whites voted then so must all
blacks; their votes were as necessary as their muskets. He
believed that the nation was bound to be just, or the war
meant little. The Radicals took the ground that now was
the time for a total rescinding of the slave tradition. The
South, they averred, should be treated as a series of conquered provinces. Military men who led the Union forces
must become governors of these Southern districts and
they should stay there until the South changed and the
Negroes were truly freed.

With this line, which was ardently pursued for a time,
the Radical Republicans became the great arm of black
liberation for as long as that resolve lasted.

But it was the Confederate force which seized the post-
bellum initiative in the period immediately after Lincoln's slaying.

Negro enfranchisement was the primary controversy
of these months in the South. Should the Negro be allowed to vote? How would one keep the vote from him?
The antislavery magazine *The Nation* sent newspaper-
man John R. Dennett to the South to report the turmoil.
Dennett reported that the immediate voting right was
crucial to the future of the country, in particular vital to
the freedman's advance, for without it "they would have
no protection against rapacity and oppression. They
would always be kept in poverty and ignorance." It was
an early forecast of what the following century would
bring.

In Andrew Johnson, a Tennesseean who began life as a tailor and taught himself politics and law, there lay concealed an unknown equation. He was supposed to be a hater of the slavocracy; he had denounced slaveholding as traitorous. But he had no love for the colored. He contained exactly the same ambivalence as seems to have characterised so many American statesmen and politicians and all of the Presidents. But he worked with force and independence. His opponents could eventually move to impeach him, but they could not influence him.

His first moves, after he assumed the Presidency, were directed toward restoring white rule over the blacks in the South. He opposed the relief assistance being given the freedmen through the Freedmen's Aid Bureau on grounds that the Negroes ought to take care of themselves.

A few weeks after the events at Ford's Theatre, the new President recognized the state governments in four Lincoln-reconstructed states. He also offered an amnesty to most inhabitants of the seven states which had not yet been recomposed by Lincoln at the time of his assassination, the amnesty that directed each of the states to repudiate the state's war debt, to abolish slavery, to elect new state governments. Each state was permitted to decide the nature of its own suffrage. That was the voting right, crucial in the freedom or slavery of anyone, and it meant that these states were being granted the right to cancel a large part of the later objectives of the war, the political elevation of the Negroes.

At once, while the North was powerless to intervene, for the soldiers had left the field and Congress was not in session, the amnestied states moved to rebuild themselves along the lines upon which they had always been constructed—as white supremacist communities.

By December of 1865, the South was legally redesigned for a continuation of about the same sectional rule as existed before the war!

During that period all of these states except Texas enacted "Black Codes." These codes, though varying somewhat from state to state, in the main militated against any real Negro advance out of slavery. The laws prohibited the colored from holding office, from serving on juries, from bearing arms; they limited property rights for Negroes, and they struck at perhaps the most fundamental human right of all, the right of the freedman to work as an artisan, a mechanic, a skilled worker. Such codes meant that the ex-slave could not enter the wage system of free enterprise, which Northern business and the Radical Republicans intended installing in the South. What the codes disallowed included many of the main reasons why the war was fought.

This precipitate rejection of emancipation by the slave states was tactless and defiant. It roused the wrath of the Radical Republicans who asserted that the South wasn't sufficiently affected by the surrender at Appomattox. The Republicans decided that they would move against such reaction when Congress resumed and when they hoped to be in control.

Out of that two-thirds of a year in the womb of a faltering Reconstruction came a portion of the monster of the new forms of white supremacy: coding, caste-ing, categorizing, limiting of the black. Out of the national failure to have a way of healing the sectional wound, of re-educating the white Southerner, of advancing the black person, and of further enlightening the Northerner —out of this frenetic time there came those fundamental rearrangements which persist until now.

It is anomalous that what occurred was the opposite of what was conveyed by Lincoln's words as to binding up the nation's wounds. He had called for malice toward none, charity for all, and for doing all that might be done toward achieving and cherishing a just and lasting peace. These sentiments were swept away by John Wilkes Booth, by Andrew Johnson, by the self-reconstructing South, by the Black Codes, by the psychological guerilla warfare (and actual warfare) that continued from 1865 on. The steadying genius, then so needed, was gone.

With malice dominant, with charity not much in existence, with the Radical Republicans fervently bent upon undoing the work of the Southern States in the post-assassination months, new American psychological outlooks began. A new white Northerner, a new white Southerner, a new-thinking black man began generating.

It is an axiom of history that economic practice and habits change the morality, mind, "heart" and general attitude of the individual. Such changes occur not only in one individual; they may encompass whole sections, nations, classes. Chattel slavery had made the slave a restless, resisting, uneducated figure who groped in religion, physical escape and revolt to change his lot. The power structure, by using science, religion, philosophy and force, had maintained its claim of organic superiority and nobility.

But new economic processes began after the Civil War, and new social attitudes were inevitable.

One of the results—and indeed unstated purposes—of the war was the destruction of the Southern economy. The South was worth about a billion dollars in banking capital at the outset of the war and it had existed primarily by a large-scale debt system. This economic complex was now shattered.

Since the South had depended for its labor supply on slaves and since they no longer had slaves, their system of producing goods was shattered. If the average value of a slave was about a thousand dollars, and four million slaves were liberated by the Emancipation Proclamation and the Thirteenth Amendment, the four billion dollar economy of the South was smashed. It meant also that this vast labor force was ready to enter the channels of America's free labor economy.

It signified a transfer of power and wealth to Northern business which would swiftly make it decisive in the world market. The South would in a few years enter into business coalitions with the North, with the North as the main profiteer. In fact, industrialization would become something of a fetish and a dream in the Southland within two or three decades. Meantime the liberation of the black man represented confiscation of human property by the North, it forecast transformation of the South, and it resulted in an irreversible but limited forward movement for the Negro laborer.

By 1865 or 1866 the Southern whites, the men women, children, and soldiers, returning from the war, faced a countryside which was impoverished, unyielding, and without any agricultural population to till the soil.

Long after the war, the towns and farms of the South contained defeated Confederate soldiers, men who were demoralised, without work and owning no property. Their bitterness remained or turned against the Negro, against the so-called carpetbagger, against the North. In some cases individuals and groups turned outlaw against either Union or section.

Others, proud Southerners, with a force tradition, a leaning to military life, their whole edifice and outlook resting upon an essential historical brutality, resumed life as men of revenge. The sodden hatred stayed within them and they developed a determination to restore themselves to rule. The South was their home, a white home in essence, they believed.

Whipped back into the Union, the "democracy" set out to renew its tradition as a separate power within the national form. The Negroes looked hopefully toward full realization as accepted citizens. The North resumed business as usual, for a time feeling that it was obligated to help both the white South and the Negroes.

All parties were destined to some disappointment. No one—save possibly Northern business—would secure exactly what he wished.

A counter-revolting South hastened to reorganize in the face of the approaching Republican occupation. This reviving "Southern Party" possessed a tradition of centuries of segmentation to draw upon in order to figure out how to circumvent, displace or tangentialize the Negro's drive.

The social history of man is a material force deriving from early unseen, unknown impulses. Much of the contradiction and violence of reconstruction grew from the powerful roots of "race" and the great white outnumbering North and South. It stemmed from sectional mistrust and from the persisting Confederate political organization. The roots of the developing Reconstruction period went as far back as the encapturing at the Gold Coast, as far back as the general effort from 1650 on to establish color curtains between peoples. It streamed back to the invention of the cotton gin and to the spread of a plantation economy straight across the frontier south during the 1800s. It stemmed from the rigidity of the white Southerner, from traditions of a vaunted aristocracy that claimed origins in Virginia colonial planter life two hundred years before.

Such history and such ingredients would make their appearance in the coming ten years alongside and in op-

position to the Northern-Republican-Abolitionist incapacity, in the face of that long historical experience, to
provide a workable program for lifting the black millions
into any clearcut freedom.

In March of 1865 came the Congressional creation
called the Freedmen's Bureau, primarily a relief establishment, an elementary step taken largely to prevent
Southern Negroes and whites from going hungry. During
the four years of its existence the Bureau, manned chiefly
by Northern white church and Abolitionist volunteers,
provided fifteen million rations to Negroes and five or six
million to whites. But the distribution of food was only a
measure of its influence and the variety of its occupation.

The volunteers who went South during and after the
war to do the practical work of feeding, caring for and
helping to liberate the slaves were principally white men
and women of the Northern churches. They acted as
friends, teachers, nurses; they helped resettle displaced ex-
slaves, and in some instances helped a few to go North if
that solution was expedient or practical. They operated
hospitals, treated illness in the home, gave legal advice to
freedmen.

If in the earliest days of chattel slavery the church pioneered with traders in bringing Africans to this country
on the pretext of saving souls, now, contrariwise, the
main force of the institution was in reverse. No sooner
did Union victories occur, as early as 1862, with freedmen arriving inside Union camps, than missionaries and
religious Abolitionists arrived with funds, books and Bibles. Though the Federal government lacked a long-
range plan or backed away from it, the individual volunteers understood the immediate needs and provided
them.

During the war Lincoln noted the feverish activity of many or most sections of the Northern church. He was constantly under their pressure to liberate the slaves and he knew that most of the soldiers in the field were churchgoing men. Once he expressed his appreciation of the church's part, saying, "It is no fault in others that the Methodist Church sends more soldiers to the field, more nurses to the hospitals, more prayers to Heaven, than any. God bless the Methodist Church! Bless all the Churches! And blessed be God, Who, in this our great trial, giveth us the Churches!"

The Negro's relationship to the church had been close for centuries, but in the postwar time the black man saw thousands of white churchmen come to his aid in a way to imbue or to renew faith. The church may have made its deepest imprint upon the psyche of the colored person in this trying period, for churches in the North, a few in the South and many in England and Ireland contributed money, men, Bibles and teachers to help the freedmen make beginnings in the larger American society. More than a half million dollars poured in from English churches alone.

The church contribution merged with the activity of the Abolitionists. Those who had for a generation most actively espoused the cause of the slave were now the most active in aiding in his industrial, educational and religious reconstruction. Antislavers of New England and New York State who had once been busy with protest, demonstration and publicist labors, entered fully into uplift effort. They flooded the border states and the Southern states. They were in each community, in offices or in church annexes or in the field, functioning in one way or another to elevate the freedman from his chattel status.

Northerners prominent throughout the antislavery

years headed up the American Freedmen's Aid Commission, an agency in New York which consolidated the efforts of numerous aid societies. William Lloyd Garrison was its vice-president. Its secretary was the writer, Frederick Law Olmstead. Other noted white Abolitionists and churchmen who helped raise funds and otherwise assist the freedmen were the poet William Cullen Bryant, Lyman Beecher and Phillips Brooks. The president of the Commission was Chief Justice Salmon P. Chase of the Supreme Court. These civic minded figures of the North put their time, money and energies into the vital labor of pulling the black man out of his hell.

One example of the enormous Northern church effort illustrates the scope of the church aid. The American Missionary Society in 1868 placed five hundred and thirty missionaries and teachers among the Negroes at a cost of $400,000 annually. Multiply that effort by the work of the various sects and denominations, each providing subsidy and field workers, and the scope of the reconstruction assistance may be visualised. All this as an implement to the work of the Freedmen's Bureau.

Because of the great emergency, the various church sects subordinated their private proselytizing and like a river simply poured support into the channels of freedmen.

By and large the white church of the South stayed apart from such emancipation efforts. Religionists of the Southern church swiftly fell in with the developing Confederate atmosphere of white restoration.

In the period 1865 to 1870, Negroes made an enormous stride forward; how far is difficult to estimate but in no comparable period since has such a large step forward been repeated. Negro churches which had maintained their entity through the war followed the lead of the white churchmen and entered into community work as a teaching force. The big objective was to eliminate illiteracy. Illiteracy had been utilised by the slavocracy as one of its most powerful means for keeping the slave in chains. The Reconstructionists regarded the teaching of reading and writing to be as important as feeding and clothing the freedmen. The African Methodists, as an example, from 1864 through 1868, placed 39,000 books in school libraries. It was from these books that the Negro learned to read. Such gains, made in that period, were never fully lost, even after disfranchisement.

The most enduring contribution was the establishment of seventeen land-grant schools for Negro education. Sponsored at the very beginning by the Radical Republicans, these schools were maintained and staffed by funds, teachers, books and supplies provided in good part by the Northern church. Fisk, Howard, Tuskegee, Talladega and many other Negro colleges had their inceptions from 1865 through 1875, under sponsorship of the Freedmen's Aid, the Republicans and the Christian churches. Most of this education was separatist in its result. Separatist schooling appeared to grow up automatically out of the *de facto* condition of millions of slaves precipitately needing economic help and education. Much of the education was religious. By the year 1868 the American Bible Society had distributed a million Bibles and other scriptural booklets. From the earliest educational efforts there was an objective not only of teaching the freedmen how to read and write, but by bringing the learning in the form of the Bible, to temper this teaching, perhaps to moderate the freedman as well as to free him.

The effect upon Negroes of seeing in their midst thousands of ardent white workers, convinced them that the Northern church was, with all of its splits, contradictions, defects—a friend. The Negroes knew that the liberal wings of the church had helped push Lincoln toward emancipation. They concluded that the church was a progressive force, sincerely helpful, that this was God's work, good work. For generations the Negro had placed faith in that church, in the possibility that advance of some kind would eventually come via that route. Now it appeared. Whatever the economic and political pressures of the great conflict, here in their midst, living by their side, was Christ.

When Republican Reconstruction was established, the brunt of enforcing reform laws fell primarily upon the backs and guns of the Negro militia. Except for the wavering protection from the Grant Administration, the Negro was in the unenviable position of having to guard the rebuilding and emancipating process almost wholly by himself.

In Mississippi, Texas, Arkansas and South Carolina, the militia was primarily black, but a minority of whites also served. Negro and white troops were joined in the militia of Tennessee, Louisiana and North Carolina, but this was still viewed as a "Negro militia" by Southern standards. The arrangement, even when a few whites served or led, tended to give the impression to the general Southern populace that the guard was all-Negro.

Not at the outset, but after a time, and in the nature of the South, the white content of the militia fell away and a virtually all-black militia was in the streets. Though some whites participated in the guard system, often in leadership capacities, they drifted out of a militia intended to crush or tame or contend with a recrudescing Confederacy.

As Northern business tried to introduce wage labor into the South—the South called that carpet-bagging—

and as black and white competed for jobs, it was a function of the militia to guard the rights of the freedmen. The militia were stationed at polling places at voting time to assure the freedmen they could vote and that their votes would be properly counted.

Any able-bodied male who did not serve in the militia was unpopular with colored women. The women, recognizing that their gains must be guarded, goaded their men to stand firm through the trying time, to shoulder arms, to withstand the constant harassment of the commando-type Confederacy organization which sprang up on all sides to destroy the militia and the Reconstruction.

The spectacle of armed black soldiers wearing the uniform of the Union, most of them veterans and crack shots now guarding arsenals, voting booths and standing at all of the State Capitol buildings, exacerbated the feelings of the already humiliated and defeated Southerners. Fear of black supremacy became widespread. Equality was also feared. There was fright at the prospect of blacks receiving the same wages for their labor as white men.

All this confirmed how sadly lacking was the nation in any operable program for truly elevating and protecting the Negroes, for re-educating the whites, for trying to set up a new, working Southern society. Little was conducive to harmony between the two peoples.

Each side worked pragmatically, making its own way day by day, each struggling for hegemony. This was an unplanned state of affairs. The colored soldiers kept it going as well as they could, but an increasing organization of whites was slowly but surely gaining strength, waiting for the weakening of Northern support for Reconstruction, paving the way for restoration of white rule.

Time played on the side of the Southern restorationists. Over the years the black militia weakened on the inside. Often the men served for months without pay. The militia was political as well as military; its political symbolism and activity made it doubly despised. Its entire meaning was Black Advance. Only arms seemed able to keep the Negro in a politically secure position so he could vote, take part in the state governments, keep schools open, and enforce the labor and other civil rights reforms that went with Reconstruction.

The main task of the regirding South, then, was to smash the black militia.

The Conservatives girded in numerous ways and through numerous organizations to decimate the militia. The first and most obvious method was simply to shoot and kill its members whenever they could be found privately, in their own homes, or off duty. It was the militia men who became primarily the lynched in this period. Constant murder of militia men, especially black officers, had the effect of weakening morale.

The assault of the Southern counter-revolt against the Reconstruction Government was of a guerilla character, an operation of political, psychological and military nature. It was a "spontaneity" born of tradition, custom, and an emotional cohesiveness developed in the Civil War. Local resistance leagues sprang up all over the South. Resistance became a contagion and a whole system of local organizations, each of racial-military character, sprouted simultaneously with a drive that would mean eventual disaster for the Reconstruction. They called themselves by romantic and dramatic, even by prosaic and innocent names: The White Liners, Jayhawkers, Ku Klux Klan, Black Horse Cavalry, Pale Faces, Knights of the White Camellia, the Constitutional Union Guards, Rifle Clubs, Council of Safety, the 1776 Association. They multiplied and communicated in a way so as to constitute an army and a legion with as much impact, retaliation and vigor as the Confederate Army itself. It *was* the Confederate Army. It was the same army reorganised, reconstituted upon local lines, and entering the field to stay until the Northern-installed Government would be harassed out of the South.

After a while democracy in the South, conservative or actually reactionary, coalesced into a system of vigilante, counter-revolutionary organizations. They were all illegal and dedicated to weakening and finally to destroying and replacing the colored militia. As a result, from the outset of the liberation period, a burgeoning system of white supremacy organizations engaged in an enfilading movement which attacked the Reconstruction in all of its manifestations: in education, in state political power, in finance, in labor.

Confident that the Confederacy would win the war of Reconstruction, inspired by the belief that a whole nation North and South would need a racial rationale, the scientists of caste and color labored with the zeal of priests and angels to pave the white wave of the future.

Literature was ready and waiting for the Klan-type organization that leaped hydra-headed to the surface of each Southern community. Neo-Confederates, embraced newly worked-out racial science as they might a beloved child. The word Race began to loom large; racial epithets were boiled down to cryptic slogans intended to steal white away from black forever and congeal the mind of each. Unable any longer to find in Christian theology an excuse for enslavement and unable to find a defense in the new wage-labor economy which supposedly was to be established in the South, the restorationists with a need born of their desperation turned to the simple clear-cut conclusions of the Southern "ethnologists." In 1869 one J. R. Hayes contributed to the controversy with the frenetically titled book issued in Washington, *Negrophobia "On the Brain." An Essay Upon the Negro Race.*

The Klansmen, the men in the White League, the White Line, the Sabre Clubs, Peoples Club, Red Shirts and White Man's Party, all these imaginative, secretive, cleverly titled groups drew upon the fifty-year-old findings of the "scientists". Books of Cartwright, Morton, Nott, de Gobineau, authors who formed a new militia of the mind, found circulation in the New Kultur of the South. The ideological fortification, in combination with practical organization against the Negro, resulted in the development of a new racial emotionalism that out-paced anything which transpired during chattel slavery. The new mysticism had the inspiration of the bitterness of defeat; it was fed by the inflaming sight of Negro militia; it was perplexed and fanned by the constant phalanx of white sympathizers of the North and many of the South who sought to guard the emancipation gains for and with the Negro.

The rhetoric of supremacy filled the air like buckshot. By the time the unpacified Confederacy sought to overthrow Reconstruction they knew exactly how to use the developed semantics of race, types, species, blood. An editorial in the *Independent Monitor* declared: "Let every man at the South through whose veins the unalloyed Caucasian blood courses, who is not a vile adventurer or carpetbagger, forthwith align himself in the rapidly increasing ranks of his species, so that we may the sooner overwhelmingly crush, with one mighty blow, the preposterous wicked dogma of Negro equality."

The innocent-sounding Sabre Club, political and military at the same time, covered 290 rifle clubs in South Carolina alone. A Congressional source reported that one-half of the white community of voting age in Mississippi was in the rifle club movement. They owned every kind of weapon used in the late war. This rearming process, which threw out the Reconstruction Government, destroyed the Negro militia, and brought the return of supremacist rule, was a full-scale military plan almost as comprehensive as the secession from the Union. The military buildup all across the South in this period went on from 1865 through 1877. It became so widespread by the early 1870s that the membership of this "New South" was as well armed as was the Confederate soldier in the war itself. But the warfare consisted of sporadic, constant, harassing engagements: individual killings, small massacres, raids on State Houses, riots, provocations, demonstrations and steady shooting at Negroes, Radicals, Republicans and the Republican State Governments.

Whatever gains the black man made in this period he engineered while a steady fusillade of gunfire came at him in town after town, state after state. The white South *never* stopped fighting against emancipation.

Advances the Negro made in education, land ownership, housing, voting and jury trial rights went on amid this incessant counter-fire. In the *Congressional Record* of the 44th Congress there is the letter to the Radical Governor Ames of Louisiana: "Dear Governor: We here give you notice that the white people of this towne have jest receved, by express from New Orleans, three boxes of guns and also some boxes of pistols for the porpus of a riot in this place."

There were two thousand men in the New Orleans League. Two-thirds of them had Belgian muskets bought in New York; most had pistols; and the club had two cannon. Yazoo City was the scene of a riot on September 1st, 1875, and A. T. Morgan, a leading Radical, described the city's military strength as he saw it from where he was hiding. He reported the soldiers were as well-armed and under as perfect discipline as any troops in the late armies. They had Winchester rifles, needle guns, double-barreled shotguns, and cavalry.

The same conditions prevailed in each of the Southern states. There was a riot in Vicksburg in which 160 armed whites from Louisiana crossed the Mississippi River to give assistance. A wire was received from Trinity, Texas: *To President Board of Supervisors: Do you want any men. Can raise good crowd within twenty four hours to kill out your negroes.*

Unlike the period of chattel slavery when the Negro had some protection because he had a value of one or two thousand dollars and could work, he was now no longer a slave, no longer anyone's private property, and he was eligible for the same treatment as the bison and the Indian. That was the line of one entire wing of the newly conceiving Southern Democracy: extermination.

The Ku Klux Klan and its ritual appealed to a mind rapidly tribalizing itself, or already consanguineous. It was the means by which whiteness was poured into the Dixie psyche and made into a morality, a virtue, a way of life. It was a form of control and a means of reducing black power; it was also a further means of buoying shattered white pride. The Southerner blamed the black for his troubles; he turned his force upon the Negro because of what he conceived to be his victimization at the hands of the Yankee.

If there had ever been much of a benevolent-patronizing-affectional relationship between master and house servant before the Civil War—and such relationships have been claimed—this diminished or vanished in the bitter postwar years.

An expert on the Southern mind, himself a Southerner with a great compassion for the defeated whites, W. J. Cash, in his *The Mind of the South,* said: "Wholly apart from the strict question of right and wrong, it is plain that slavery was inescapably brutal and ugly. Granted the existence in the higher levels, of genuine humanity of feeling toward the bondsman; granted that, in the case of the house-servants at least, there was sometimes real affection between master and slave; granted even that at its best, the relationship here got to be gentler than it has ever been elsewhere, the stark fact remains: It rested on force. The lash lurked always in the background. Its open crackle could often be heard where field hands were quartered . . . And in the common whites it bred a savage and ignoble hate for the Negro, which required only opportunity to break forth in relentless ferocity."

What had been true of the period of chattel slavery became a more frozen truth in Reconstruction.

As the revived Confederacy, in the guise of its various social clubs and sabre clubs, made their steady inroads, the policy of President Grant and of the Republican Federal Government became more and more *laissez faire*. The chattel slave system had been destroyed and it no longer stood in the way of the advance westward or of insuring Northern banking and industrial influence in Washington.

Grant said he was tired of the annual autumnal outbreaks of black-white hostility in the Reconstruction states. In critical engagements when the military Democrats were about to seize the State Governments away from the Reconstruction Generals, the Federal Government would not back up the beseiged Reconstruction forces with troops. The racists learned that the North was tiring of the situation in the South and going its own way; they took heart and intensified military pressure.

The counter-attack which began perhaps within moments or hours of Appomattox bore fruit within four years in Tennessee. By that time whites were in full repossession of their government and state. During the next five years the Democrats in Virginia, Georgia, North Carolina, Alabama, Arkansas and Texas regained control of their state apparatus. In 1875, crisis in Mississippi and failure of the Grant Administration to help with Federal troops, resulted in restoration in that state. So-called redemption occurred in Florida, Louisiana and South Carolina later.

In this period a cry of the conservative Democratic polity was that the Reconstruction governments were corrupt and dishonest. But the charge of dishonesty and corruption had nothing to do with the home rulers' desire or need or purpose in trying to recapture Southern control. This was mostly ruse and rationalization intended to weaken Northern support of the Reconstruction Governments. It was only specious argument intended to act as one more reason for white reaccession to power. It was a charge seized upon by the guerilla political operators of the neo-Confederacy intended to affect religionist groups North and South. It was simply another gun, one used in the propaganda warfare that went along with the military warfare.

But the North, to cover up for its loss of interest in the Reconstruction cause, welcomed and repeated these charges as if this were the reason white home rule should be restored.

The real reason was simple: traditional, racial-national retaliation, aspiration and determination. Yet to the present day, in books used in schools throughout the United States, historians veer away from the essential supremacist motivations that are endemic to the nation's total history from 1619 on.

The Civil War, and thereafter the bloody Reconstruc-

tion, congealed for many millions that sovereign color-
ness that went back to William Penn who owned slaves,
to one Puritan preacher after another who could see little
or nothing wrong in slavery; it went back to and it extended from Episcopal Church Bishop Polk of Louisiana
who, just before the war, owned four hundred slaves.

The amazing thing is that in the face of this the Negro
could consolidate at all, that he could make his quasi
gains, that he could fight for time in the face of this
avalanche, that he became literate, that he retained political entity and identity, that he even acquired property. It
was remarkable that he in this period secured a foothold
in the democracy, one that he would never fully lose.
This may have been his prime achievement in the thirty
years that succeeded the war: that in spite of his blood-
shed, gain was made, ground was held.

Meantime the Northern public developed an immunity
to reports of atrocities to Negroes. The story of calamity,
death, segregation, insult, was old by now; they had
heard it in chattel slavery, during the war, now it continued; and in the South among so-called Caucasians there
had always been such an inurement that it was possible
by attrition alone for a Democratic South to tap this
chronic chord in the national temper and to recreate an
atmosphere in both sections in which persecution was
tolerated. The philosophic anomaly underlying the process was that this new Southern society, moving into a
special brand of American totalitarianism, described itself as "Democrat."

In the North, the old gambit of getting rich, the
quicker the better, and forgetting war, was in full harness
by 1874 and 1875. In Northern states large numbers
wanted peace, prosperity, avoidance of sectional issues.

Conservative interests became increasingly impervious to the constant report of Southern difficulties. The scene itself was changing: urbanization leaped forward as new millions entered the nation from Europe. Labor in the North confronted capital. White labor was fighting for the eight-hour day. Ideas like socialism, anarchism, syndicalism were in the air. In front of factories there were picket lines. An organization called the Knights of Labor was in the field and making impact on free enterprise relations. White labor wasn't thinking much of the black man's problems. And as urbanization developed, hundreds of thousands of Europeans were settling in Western states, starting farms, establishing new markets. The countryside bloomed with the products of the energies of the new farming populations. Trade between the East and the West increased. In Chicago a great meat industry developed. Railroads chugged from coast to coast. And as these changes took place in the North, in the East, the Middle West and the West, the Southern states continued their vertical struggle, with man fighting man, with racial thinking still the dominant mode.

As war recollections went into books, memoirs, annual celebrations, and into endless re-play of the battles over crackerbarrel sessions, the main mass from New York to California was bent upon individual survival, private advance—a principal social occupation of mankind in all ages. The term "rugged individualism" was heard. The magical names J. P. Morgan, Andrew Carnegie, John D. Rockefeller, became the idols of a money-worshipping community, replacing the Civil War Generals who were getting the monuments while the industrialists were reaping the emoluments.

Not blood was wanted now, but oil.

Petroleum was discovered; its manifold uses were being exploited. Thomas Edison would initiate the age of electrical application. With spectacles like this, and progress like that, let the South handle its own affairs in its own way. This developing "leave them alone" policy went back several years; it began soon after the Civil War. As early as 1872 Horace Greeley, founder of the Republican Herald-Tribune, most noted antislavery editorial writer, became the Democratic candidate for President. The cycle had started turning early and swiftly. Opportunism became the Reconstruction's other spirit, symbol, sign and destination.

Rutherford B. Hayes, the Republican candidate for the Presidency in 1876, was born and reared in Ohio. He had been a Union general in the Civil War and after the war he seemed to have profound sympathies for the freedmen; when he ran for governor of Ohio in 1867, he expressed the thought that the exclusion of the Negro population from a full part in Government was a monstrous inconsistency, an injustice, an impossibility.

Yet as men rise in politics and their glance falls upon the White House, they often change; their liberalism modifies; their capacity for compromise grows.

By the time he accepted the Republican nomination he began temporising with the meaning of the Constitution, referring to the "hearty and generous recognition of the rights of all"—by which it turned out that he meant the rights of the Southern conservative Democracy. Appealing to a widely developed sentiment in the North for the closing out of the sectional strife, he intimated that Federal Government ought to help states—by which he meant the Southern states—to work out their fates by themselves, "to obtain for themselves the blessings of honest and capable government."

He and his party held out a promise of compromise,

abandonment of Black Reconstruction while at the same time throwing rhetorical bouquets at "the rights of all," which could even mean the freedmen.

Some historians contend that the nation faced another civil war in the 1870s, that the South had regirded, rearmed sufficiently to secede again, and it has been held that Hayes was compelled to put forward a policy of pacification to prevent a recurrence of war.

When the Presidential elections took place in the fall of 1876, it appeared that Hayes was narrowly defeated by the Southern Democratic candidate, Samuel Tilden. As Republicans challenged the determination at the polls, the issue of who should be President turned into a conflict within the Electoral College, as well as in Congress. Questions of legality, of the honesty of the voting, the counting of ballots—all became locked in a new controversy. This one was destined to be a high level decision worked out behind the scenes, a deal tinged with the backroom aroma of Southern magnolias.

Throughout his campaign Hayes had promised the South that if he were elected he would introduce a spirit of compromise; he implied that he would withdraw federal troops, he would honor local rule and states rights, he would let the South go it alone and handle the black man in its own way. He didn't put it quite as openly as that. With the finesse of all men skilled in public life he used rhetoric cloaked in allusions that must be interpreted. In high phrases he spoke of the strides the Negro was making and expressed hope and belief that this would continue.

Much jockeying went on between the Northern and Southern politicians during the critical period from that election through late February of 1877. The railroad lobby entered into talks with Southern business men and leaders, with a plan to arrange for the building of a

Texas and Pacific railroad line. In return, Hayes would become President, would at once withdraw federal troops from the South, and Northern and Southern business would get together. The federal subsidy never materialised, but the rest of it did.

A nodal point in the transformation of American psychology, of both the white and the black, occurred as a consequence of the famous Wormley Hotel Conference in Washington on February 26th and 27th, 1877.

It is a searing oddity of history that a civil war of prolonged duration, with so much slaughter, followed by ten years of liberal struggle for some equalization of the human conditions, for Negroes and whites, could be all but cancelled out in two days by the connivances of a handful of Northern and Southern politicians. It is a paradox, not at all peculiar to politics that without even signing a paper of agreement for history to examine, two compromising parties could, over a few luncheons, reject and rearrange the past, the struggle, the Emancipation Proclamation, the address at Gettysburg. The future was sold out in a smoke-filled room.

Anomalous or not, such smoke-filled hotel rooms have produced more changes of American history, more alterations of living for millions of people, than have been produced by all the prior smoke-filled battlefields. After the Wormley Hotel meetings, the cynicism of the long-corrupted politicians, the weariness of the North, the desperation of the South, and business competition in both sections, could achieve a sectional compromise, that partially undid a century of struggle and at the same time ushered in another century of conflict. A generation could lay down its life for a cause, while in a two-day spasm of agreement, promises, handshaking and double-dealing, a small band of men could vitiate the meanin of that history. The pawn in such a chess game was of course the possession of the high office of the Presidency. How tragic that human ambition could, in such a crisis, write off Lincoln and the constitutional amendments that followed upon the great Emancipator's works.

Soon after Hayes was inaugurated President he proceeded to withdraw troops from two Southern states. He ordered the return to the North of 34 officers and 316 enlisted men in South Carolina on April 10th; and ten days later he ordered 22 officers and 271 enlisted men located at New Orleans to be withdrawn. Hayes worked on the supposition that the restored Southern Democrat governments would protect freedmen's rights. Had they not promised to do so? The process of expelling the Reconstruction Governments, begun earlier by the South, was completed by the Federal Government. Later, Hayes took an olive branch trip through the Southern states. He talked of good will, he urged the South to obey the Thirteenth, Fourteenth and Fifteenth Amendments. Actually he only hardened the cement of restoration. He was applauded everywhere, except by Negroes who were cool, polite and aware of what had happened. Ahead of the black people now was a long pull against a combined North-South tide.

Despite promises of the Southern politicians to sustain the constitutional rights of the Negroes in return for removal of troops and the right to run their own state governments, within two years, as President Hayes was to discover, three-quarters of a million colored votes were disfranchised. In his second annual address in 1878 Hayes mentioned Louisiana, Mississippi and South Carolina as states where Negroes were violently defrauded of voting rights. Negroes had been driven from the polls, many were beaten, a few killed, others frightened away.

So serious was the reaction against the Negroes, after

the compromise, that during the years 1878 and 1879 more than 40,000 Negroes moved North and West to hopefully more liberal regions.

In 1879, when it was known all over Europe that a counter-revolution had succeeded in the United States, the Czar of Russia, Alexander II, claimed that the lack of a program in Lincoln's Emancipation Proclamation prepared the way for the disasters of Reconstruction. The Czar said that when he emancipated the serfs he gave them land and the tools with which to work the land; but the Negroes had been given only an expulsive freedom which removed them from plantations but did not supply them with the means for making a productive life for themselves. It was in large measure true: the freedman was not admitted in any clear-cut way to the free labor economy and the result was that the compromise semi-serfdom of the sharecropping system developed.

This was an economy of indebtedness in which the worker, black or white, tilled the soil, "shared" its product with the plantation owner. But it was a limping economy that impoverished all connected with it.

The ambivalence expressed by President Hayes in public statements as well as official actions more or less set the tone for Presidential aspirants, candidates and incumbents for the next generation. From that time when Republican and Democrat closed ranks there followed a tacit understanding in political campaigns and in Congress that lip service must always be paid full rights for Negroes but in actuality these must never be accorded by either Republican or Democrat.

After Hayes came Presidents Garfield, Arthur, Cleveland and Harrison. With each there arrived tons of campaign rhetoric promising full freedom for Negroes, plus restoration of voting rights, but in practice there was only steady deterioration of the voting right.

Southern policy on state and national levels was everywhere the same. It held to a line first expressed by Governor Wade Hampton of South Carolina during President Hayes' tour of the South. Hampton, in a speech at Louisville, Kentucky, said that the Federal Constitution was being observed in the South and that it always would be. This statement became from then on a fixture in Southern politics. Democrats blithely announced that in their part of the world the Constitution was observed, it always would be observed, and there was no question about it. Meantime the Negro was being moved more and more out of official life. This process of bland promise became characteristic of so-called racial politics North and South; it added to the cynicism of politics in general. It has since been accepted as a "principle" in national politics that the public expects to find a disparity between promise and application.

Under President McKinley the plight of the Negro worsened. Pressure of international affairs made it possible for that administration to sublimate the color question entirely. From 1892 through 1898, the two administrations of McKinley, "sectional harmony" was complete and a reality. The peace of the South was a white peace. Separation of white and black was as inviolable as the patterns of day and night. Lynching, riots, beatings and disfranchisement went on through the McKinley administrations while, in the North, press and politics either remained mute to the protestations of the black, or raised higher the banner proclaiming the right of Southern states to rule themselves. The Negro occupied a position best described in 1881 by President Garfield who, in a bold echoing of the old Republican tradition remarked,

"There can be no permanent disfranchised peasantry in the United States."

But there was. And it developed even more sharply in the twenty years that followed that statement.

By 1900 the black man on the plantations had reached the condition of a voteless peasant. He was little better off in the urban centers of the North. He had become a forgotten man, about whom public pronouncement was rare; but in private action, on the roads of the South, he became the victim of the new post-bellum technique called lynching.

From the 1880's onward there was talk of anti-lynching legislation. The black man's condition had changed from the time of Emancipation when the issue was how to secure full rights for the Negro people. Now the maximum advocacy was not full rights at all, but simply to halt lynching. And that legislation couldn't be passed.

What was happening was a general sliding backward through time, back to an alien status, to a condition only a twisted notch or two beyond the chattel slave's status.

On the Negro's part there was a gigantic effort to save whatever could be saved of the gains of Reconstruction. Mainly this was the system of segregated schools. But it was difficult to survive in the new Southland where every white man was an unofficial policeman. The Negro groped to find ways out. Flight to the North was one resort. Some in the 1880s and 1890s seriously considered setting up a black republic in the Far Northwest, of migrating there and establishing their own economy. But no financing was available for such a move. Still, there began that steady flow of individuals and families out of the South which has continued to this day: and nothing has proved the absolutism of the South then and now with any more conviction than this never-ending migration. The black man found in mobility, change of scene and penetration of places in the North and West some surcease from the indignities free men did not have to endure.

Everything in the Southern syndrome, its steady political disfranchisement of the Negro; its continuous self-generating thesis that Anglo-Saxon raciality must be preserved and extended; its thesis that the North did not understand the Southern white or Negro; the continuous spread of segregation—all this tended toward a deepening concept of caste.

The bifurcation of peoples found expression in the words of Henry Grady, the Atlanta journalist and spokesman for the restored Democracy, who advised Negroes to adjure Northern, Republican and radical support and to throw in their lot with the tender mercy of the Southern white man. Grady, in public speeches, in magazine articles, in editorials written for the *Atlanta Constitution,* projected the idea that Negro prosperity depended upon the affluence of his white masters with whom he lived and for whom he worked. Grady convinced whites, if not the Negroes, that in general all was well in the South, a *detente* was in effect, the black man was progressing, the white role was ameliorating.

Grady's theme had been uttered by many other Southerners as far back as the early days of Reconstruction. A theory that black and white could and would harmonize in the South if only the black recognized his place had been softly and eloquently placed before the public North and South for decades.

Booker T. Washington made his famous speech in Atlanta, Georgia, on September 18th, 1895, in which he said: "In all things that are purely social we can be as separate as the fingers, yet one as the hand in all things essential to mutual progress."

Actually Washington had not invented a thing. He had picked up what was in the air and what had been in the Southern air for a generation. He repeated and reflected others; but he by no means devised the separate society idea. That was conceived by a whole line of observers before him.

As throughout the history of the Negro, the status of the black man was still being invented, arranged and reoriented exclusively by the whites, and over the resistant pressure of the black.

Yet when Washington made his utterance it was received everywhere not as accommodation to an already enunciated white policy, but as if it were a policy devised by Washington himself. North and South leaped to congratulate him as a statesman. Still, Washington's acceptance and projection of the "separate as the fingers" line merely represented another demarcation point in the long tough struggle of the black man.

And it is a matter of record that when Washington delivered his address, a reporter for the *New York World* remarked that many of the Negroes in the audience were crying. A sad moment of further official parting of the races had arrived and the Negroes present realized the significance.

In the North inventive genius was in general encouraged, recognized and advanced, but this was hardly so in the South.

Significant creativity centered largely around figuring out some new place to put up a "White Only" or "Colored Only" sign. This game occupied the energies of thousands of civic officials for about two generations. A type of caste-system cartography developed.

Lines of demarcation were established in every city and village directing where white could go and black could not, where white could drink or eat or defecate, and where the Afro-American could not. The social checkerboard born of white prejudice covered the whole South. It became a maze through which black and white must wander forever at arm's length, God's children who must not touch each other's hands.

A thousand means, devices, techniques, experiments throughout the South and as far north as New Jersey, occupied in the most dedicated way the earnest creative attention of politicians, civic figures, administrators, police and intellectuals. A hundred thousand white men painted the little signs that went up in hotels, trains, schools, public buildings. They were established with the same religiosity with which the Confederate flag was everywhere flown.

Separate and inequal—separate toilets, separate drinking fountains, separate pews, and separate seats on public transportation. This segregation process, devised around the 1890's, spread like hot white fire across the South by the year 1900. It systematized segregation. It had an aura of completion, of simple totalitarianism. In that half of territorial America black and white must pass and circumvent each other according to a brand new charted universe—segregated neighborhoods, separate schools, segregated Gods.

The psychological effect was vast. It separated minds, hearts, bodies. The single act of denoting where white could and could not pass and where black could pass and could not pass, produced an estrangement of incomparable dimension. These intersecting do's and don'ts determined the thinking of nearly everybody Southside; it became known as the Jim Crow System. By 1910, it began to look as if it had existed for a million years. Southern "genius" had constructed a wall better than the Chinese a thousand years earlier, a wall built with bricks of fear and ignorance.

If it were possible to gather a printed record of all the state and local regulations determining segregation patterns, the listing would require a lawbook the size of a trunk. A few of the titles illustrate the enormity of this codification: *Black Laws of Virginia, Legal Status of the Negro, Judicial Decisions Concerning the Negro,* and so on through the records which have catalogued the ingenuity of the nonblack through the American age.

Although such rules began as early as the 1600s, one of the busiest periods of all for the institution of such coding was the relatively recent period of Woodrow Wilson's Presidency—not through his instigation nor because he in any way opposed the lawmaking, but because it was a final ram-through period, an opaque era of profound suppression. In the North, Yankee inventive ingenuity reached an advanced state. And in the South mechanical instinct continued in its private Poe-like dream world, seeking new zones into which black could not go.

Of all the legalities most deeply altering the mores of white and black, those having the most to do with building the national neurosis were the rulings in two-thirds of the states of the Union against intermarriage and cohabitation of the sexes of opposite color. Beyond separating opposite sexes of black and white, the pervasive spread of this moved out to include in many states Mongols, Hindus, Malays, "Orientals," and American Indians.

Intermarriage bans became the archstone of the design intended to keep black and white apart. This was never confined to the South, but also involved the entire West as far north as Oregon and Montana. The way in which a large part of the country North and South has worked at color restrictions accounts for the stubbornness of the alienations; it explains why the transfer of large black populations into Northern ghettos has been accompanied by or followed by experiences in antagonism in the North comparable with that belonging to the traditional South. With time thirty-six states prohibited marriage between white and Negro. A typical punishment for such a transgression was confinement in a penitentiary for two to five years. For ministers or others who presided over such marriages jail sentences and fines were established. In South Carolina a Negro minister could marry Negro couples, but not the white. In Maryland the law said that any white woman who became pregnant by a Negro or a mulatto would go to prison for five years.

Laws on the books in various states now rule against more than two-thirds of the world's population—Asiatics, Africans, South Americans. Fifteen Far Western states have laws opposing marriage between Chinese and Caucasians; whites and Malays cannot marry in some ten states; whites and Indians may not marry in at least five states; Indians and Negroes cannot marry in Louisiana and Oklahoma.

The nation had traveled a long way from its inceptions when separation of the colors was for purposes of maintaining a reservoir of cheap labor. Now such emotion had entered the two-group relationships that original economic motivations became partially lost in the heated racial atmosphere. The consequence of black codes, established as part of what the South called "the struggle for racial purity," was that an actual asexuality was achieved for millions of males and females. Fear of punishment, ostracism, violation of the social code rose to such intensity on both sides that the sexes of opposite colors come to fear even looking at one another. Men and women might pass each other on the street, and if of different colors, no sexual chord passed between them. "Race awareness" was the active emotion. So complete was the organization of such alienation, caste and class fear, so well worked out the estrangement, that in millions of instances men and women would feel no human attraction, but perhaps even repulsion. The law bade it so, made it so.

In spite of this enormous coding process, national rather than regional, there was a tacit "escape clause" in the system for white men. The law blinked its eye if the white man had relations with a woman of color. This tolerance, this exception, which holds even now in all sections, had its root in the slave period when masters sired slaves by Negro women, watched their mixed children move around their plantations, took pride in it when the progeny looked like the master, then sold their own progeny into slavery: a paternalistic ritual found in modern times solely in the history of the white men.

But in the 1890s there was a moment of continuity in the course of what might be called exclusively Negro history, if such there can be in a nation where black and white have been so indissolubly interlinked by labor and procreative history. The Abolitionist leader, Frederick Douglass, was Minister to Haiti and married to a white woman; his successor in the new period of accommodation, Booker T. Washington, had gained the favor of the ruling classes North and South. Each had in common the fact that he did not know his white father. Douglass said he knew nothing of his, that slavery had no recognition of fathers and none of families. Booker Washington said he understood that his father was a white man who lived on a nearby plantation, but if it were true, this man never took any interest in his son. In Washington's case he found no fault with that remission saying that his father was "simply another unfortunate victim of the institution which the Nation unhappily had engrafted upon it at that time."

The prime objective of the legislative process was to prevent the black man from mingling with or marrying the white women. This was the uttermost need of an economy and a philosophy of cultural superiority. In the South this condition was dubbed by W. J. Cash as "the rape complex." Each white man had to believe that any and all Negroes were a threat to any and all white women. Only the intermarriage laws rigidly enforced by occasional violence would keep the white woman and the black man apart. Out of this anti-biological crusade the most impossible gulf was established. It took seventy-five years to complete it. The preconditions for this schism were there in slavery, but it was hardened at the opening of this century, and it remains general now.

As lynch law evolved to back up the codes, the alienation reached such a stage of breadth that even large numbers of white men in the South would not venture across the line. When this occurred asexuality was as complete as it could be and the officialdom had about perfected its task of color separation.

In spite of this alienation and asexuality, an ambiguous byproduct is that each color group has developed fantasy patterns about the sexual endowment of the other. This has led to a whole mythology of belief, conviction and curiosity. The opposite sex of the other color may be fancied a superior or more exciting sex mate. The black woman, aware of the ruling economic and social status of the white man, may be tempted into sexual or emotional attachment, not because the white is any better as a lover, but the social position he occupies connotes warmth, ease, security, acceptance, and hence emotional satisfaction. In that case superior status may be equated with sex desirability. White men, having been taught that there is a "primitivism" in the black woman, may fancy her to be a less inhibited figure than her white sister. The black man, primary victim of isolation, cannot forget the protective arrangement around the white woman, the danger of prison and lynching if he transgresses the code. Here the patterns grow psychologically confused, unreal for all parties concerned; it is a sex syndrome troubled by misunderstanding, social distance, myth, slander, and terror.

INTO THE PRESENT CENTURY

A new nation, a Southern nation, was formed in these years. Stretching from the Atlantic through Texas, it was conceived, built, created on the simple premise that all white men had in common their pigment and therefore, a human right of superiority, and that the black population of the South must resign itself to an inferior self-contained caste condition for all time.

White superiority intensified. The violence of the Klan merged with the legal apparatus of the White Primary and the Democratic Party. Here the congealment acquired a character of absoluteness.

The building of the Southern wing of the Democratic Party was the final stage of all in the development of a clear, definitive race prejudice. Now the attitude of superiority had the sanction of total political philosophy. The Democratic Party, built upon new oppression of the black, was sure that it could take hold of the political processes and climb back to power, and did so. It perfected a school of loud, boisterous white supremacist politicians on the order of the late Eugene Talmadge, along with Senatorial types who sought with oratory and filibuster and maneuver to maintain reborn southern philosophy.

As a result of the South's overwhelming effort to disfranchise the black, even poor whites lost the right to vote. The statutes of the various states became filled with provisions requiring poll-tax payment as a right to vote, educational tests of an unconscionably difficult order, and property qualifications for people who had little or no property. These regulations now militated against the poor but "superior" whites as strongly as against the colored.

At the turn of the century, the North had moved into the century of billion dollar claims, billion dollar language. The railroad system, considered the backbone of the country with its constant consumption of iron, coal, steel, was now a ten billion dollar complex. Who cared about human rights? Automobiles appeared on the market. Who cared about lynchings? Airplanes were flying, so what mattered a drinking fountain that said White and another that said Black?

There developed a widespread tendency in the North to accept ready-made the propaganda and pretensions from below the Mason-Dixon line. The South, people said, had its special concepts, some of which had their origins in the era before the Civil War. Other attitudes were new. Negroes were now viewed variously as criminals, cowards, comics, congenital rebels, Uncle Toms. Whites believed that blacks had special animal faculties —more rhythm, for example, than white people. They could sing and dance better because these were primitive gifts. Most of these ideas sprang directly from professional racists. Others were invented by the Southern press.

Caricatures of dialect appeared in newspapers, magazines and books. The power of Negro idiom and mother wit was not understood, but anything in writing which could make the English language seem to be well chopped up by colored speakers found favor with writers and readers. The Negro became the butt of jokes that circulated from person to person throughout the nation, usually based upon his real or alleged illiteracy, his physical or color characteristics, or his poverty. And white-owned newspapers in the North gave wide circulation to such jokes and anecdotes, furthering the notion of the Negro as a different, special being.

The old journals which had fought for the Negro, now staid and money-making, were directing their attention to the wonders of the fortunes which were amassing in the North. Intellectual periodicals like *The Century, Forum* and *Harper's* drifted with the new accommodation. No longer did any voice in the land sound like the early *Liberator, Scribner's* or the *Atlantic*. Other sophisticated organs of opinion took the position of letting the South handle Negroes in its own way. A favorite theme now by Southern writers in these periodicals was that Negro freedmen suffering in freedom had fared so much better under slavery.

When the United States Government at the turn of the century set up immigrant quotas based upon race and nationality, every nation in the world was aware of the flood of racist writing and speaking that went along with this step.

Author and editorialist William Allan White declared in 1899, "It is the Anglo-Saxon's manifest destiny to go forth in the world as a world conqueror. He will take possession of all the islands of the sea. He will exterminate the peoples he cannot subjugate. That is what fate holds for the chosen people. It is so written. Those who would protest will find their objections overruled. It is to be."

And eleven years later he was still saying: "The best blood of the earth is here—a variated blood of strong, indomitable men and women brought here by visions of wider lives. But this blood will remain a clean Aryan blood, because there are no hordes of inferior races about to sweep over us and debase our stock. We are separated by two oceans from the inferior races, and by that instinctive race revulsion to cross-breeding which marks the American wherever he is found."

It was racism still, white racism, stronger then ever before.

Merely by repeating and reporting the violence tradition, the press reflected the historical record and produced feelings of inevitability in white and black. By its often straightforward, noncommital reporting it added weight and point to the fact of the stamping and imprinting process: always refeeding the American brain and soul in either old or new ways. *First Negro at West Point Knifed by Fellow Cadets; Texans Lynch Wrong Negro; Negro Burned Alive in Florida; Negro Hung by Mob, Roasted Alive; Innocent Man Lynched; Mob Scares Negro Woman to Death; Innocent Man Lynched; Two Blacks Strung Up—Grave Doubt of Their Guilt; Lynched Before Trial; Hoosiers Hang Negro Slayer; Jury Commends Mob for Cremating Negro; Negro Burned at Stake; Mob Drives Negros Out, Burns Home . . .*

By and large the white had no view of himself as the Negro saw him. A hundred million whites were generally innocent of the fact that, far from being looked upon as a superior, cultured creature, the white man had become a diabolical over-image, variously a monster or a devil. The point of view from "below" was expressed in June, 1903, by Reverend Montrose Thornton, the Wilmington, Delaware, pastor of the African Methodist Episcopal Church, after a lynching: "The white man, in the face of his boasted civilization, stands before my eyes tonight the demon of the world's races, a monster incarnate, and insofar as the Negro race is concerned seems to give no quarter. The white is a heathen, a fiend, a monstrosity before God and is equal to any act in the calendar of crime. I would sooner trust myself in the den of a hyena as in his arms."

In the period of the Great Retreat, as it might be called, in a mystical fury, despair and hope, the Negro fell back upon a last but important fortification, the church. The church, which had succored the freedman after the war and the one institution into which most Negroes were organized, became the Rock. Here the Negro pastors could criticise and protest in a way not allowable in the nonchurch environment. The whites knew that the black pulpits frequently rang with denunciation of Southern oppression, but they considered it a bottled up protest limited to the interior of the church. When the protest affected jimcrow patterns, the white oligarchy became more restive and from time to time drove a Negro minister out of the South. Some whites regretted that they had allowed the Negro to develop so large an institution in which to function, but it was generally felt that the church was "safe."

From 1900 through 1930 the church in the South and in segregated districts of the North became community center, talking ground, planning ground, culture workshop, defiance center, spiritual haven, educational experience. It developed as the principal builder of Negro personalities, those who would make their appearance in public life and often before the white community.

The church became the prime political base for the Afro-American. Nobody who went into politics could get very far without having a following in the church. Church leaders for a time became the primary voice of the Afro-American, along with and through the Negro press. It became an epoch of church experiment: Negroes formed their own churches, their own religious communities; they opened little main street halls or lofts and ordained themselves ministers, pastors, evangelists.

Masters of the Bible appeared. Preachers learned to use it, to teach themselves through it and to teach others.

Poor black men thrown into Southern prisons, unable to read and write when they entered, learned there to read from the Bible. That is how several of the Scottsboro boys learned to read and write when in the 1930s they were thrown into Alabama prisons.

Methodists, Baptists, Presbyterians, Episcopalians and countless other sects fought to divide the religious preserve among them. Church feuds and splits took place among Baptists, Methodists and Presbyterians. The church became a vital bootstraps operation. Underneath the operation there was the deadly purpose of breaking through the supremacist society somehow in some way.

Up to the Civil War and for a short time thereafter the Negro church was perhaps the only structure or institution which the black possessed. After the Civil War the church acquired breadth, ramification, property, communicants and a vitality sufficient to constitute a communication system. There was a natural progression from the church into politics. Race was church and church became politics. The church leader often wound up as the race leader or spokesman, the man to negotiate with the white folks. During Reconstruction the colored ministers were considered apt candidates for political office.

Scarcely a state in the South during that time did not have some Negro ex-pastors in the state governments. A typical example of the Negro pastor in politics was the instance of Bishop B. W. Arnett, a leader of the African Methodist Church, who was elected to the Ohio Legislature from Greene County, Ohio, in 1885. Once in office he fought for repeal of the Ohio Black Laws which dated back to the slavery period. Negro preachers served influentially in Northern and Southern political office from 1865 through 1900.

Out of the spread of the church came the development of fraternal organizations, business enterprise, the own-

ership of church property, funeral businesses, food cater-
ing businesses, even banking developments. Around
church life there developed a romantic and matrimonial
meeting of the young. From local churches the young
Negroes moved into the segregated colleges. Readings in
history, the presentation of dramatics, interest in poetry
and essays, all occurred in church halls. Eloquent, highly
literate Bible teachers and pastors acted as inspiration for
young Negroes who could make no entry into the closed
white educational world: but the seed was planted for the
winning of the cultural fronts.

Out of the role of the church as the primary social-
cultural center for millions of Negroes in the first quarter
of this century came small islands of Negro intellectuals.
Public speaking, debates and oratory developed. Forums
gave opportunity to the young to discover their aptitudes,
and from these beginnings to strike out in individual directions and to attempt to crack the white world. These
influences in part led to the Negro literary renaissance of
the 1920s. Literary societies became an integral part of
the thousands of Negro churches that spread across the
Southland. Out of this environment came an interest in
sociology, in dealing with the needs of impoverished
blacks who must look to one another for succor when
care or employment was not forthcoming from the white
community. The church finally watched over practically
all phases of black life—often its music, usually its ath-
letic programs. It established day nurseries and employment bureaus. The church became the black man's world,
for he was not admitted to the white except to work and
then to return to his ghetto.

As the spiritual-political requirements of the ten millions expanded, the church became more and more the
grand bulwark of the Southern Negro. Health needs, wel-

fare services, social uplift—all facets of life stemmed from and around the religious center.

Moreover, by now a great competition developed among Baptists, Methodists, other Protestant sects and Catholics, each to have most effect, to win the most communicants, to develop the most far-reaching programs.

By the year 1906 there were more than 36,000 church organizations in the Afro-American community, with more than three and one-half million members. There were no less than 35,000 church edifices and more than 1250 halls used as places in which to worship. The church buildings alone were worth fifty-six million dollars. Ninety percent of the church organization was located in the South.

During the period from 1890 through about 1910 the white Methodist, Baptist and Lutheran churches lost most of their Negro communicants. The dissolving of white-Negro relations in virtually every area of society split up white churches, forced the blacks out and compelled them to retreat into the large-scale separation which was to characterize almost every phase of Afro-American life up through the Depression. Methodists and Baptists divided between them most of the church wealth, most of the communicants and most of the pastors. As a religious-spiritual-political life developed within these main sects, splinter Protestant groups appeared and set up their own organizations.

By the time the great seclusive Negro church blanketed community life in the South and dominated the ghetto life in the Northern cities, the institution became engaged in the fight against segregation, in raising funds for the National Association for the Advancement of Colored People and for other organizations. More Negroes were in the clergy than in any other profession.

While the entire colored family went in this huge religious-oriented direction, a comparable phenomenon was occurring in the white South: whites by the millions entered into a comparable but different seclusion, filling the white churches on Sundays.

Each Sunday for seventy years the two separate churches met on opposite sides of town filling their respective white pews and black pews. This developed into a mass mutual Sunday "demonstration," the white church demonstrating its separation from and superiority over the black in the name of Christ, and the Afro-American church demonstrating its solidarity and its protest over the white interpretation of God and Christ. The same process occurred in the North: there the masses of whites went to church all through these years generally ignorant of or indifferent to the religious life of the ghetto, yet in the main sharing with the Southern white church alienation from the Negro world.

This massive schism of black and white in the heart of God Himself became one of the prime manifestations of the Caucasian Way. It was a mode of living, thinking, worshiping in which thousands of white clergy partook, either with deliberate awareness of what they were doing, or in an innocent ignorance of how the other tenth lived.

Little in our society has illustrated the anomaly of the caste system with any greater dramatic force than this contradiction of Christianity.

By 1936 close to one-tenth of all the property owned by Negroes was in churches. By now there were about 40,000 Negro churches. In that year more than five and one-half million Negroes were enrolled. No other institutions on the black side showed any such involvement of the masses. They were not involved in political parties in any numbers; they were barely beginning to get into labor unions; and the new radical parties could claim only minute percentages of such membership figures.

During the 1920s when millions of Negroes moved North, church life moved North with them. There numerous Negroes switched churches and many approached the Catholic Church. Some alignment of Negroes and the Catholic Church occurred in the 1920s when the Klan lumped Negroes and Catholics as anathema.

A large percentage of this religious force has been quite exclusively spiritual. Many Negroes escaped from the power structure over them into an inner world of hiding from the white and in dreaming of a heaven after death. Some of this has been a faith, a praying, a philosophic certainty that life must have some real inner meaning and true value despite discrimination, segregation and humiliating caste. Many of these Negroes drifted into private realms of religious experience, and for these the mysticism of the church, a pure drift into the spirituality of Jesus, has been the meaning, the purpose and the end of the Negro church.

Thus the Church has functioned in the way all churches seem to function, in transitions from earth to heaven. Either way the Afro-American church contained and held the black soul together for so long a time.

The phenomenon of an expanding church power in Negro life complemented the continuous rejection of the black man and woman from the white power structure and superstructures. The more the barriers remained, the more impassioned and numerous became the black church membership. Quietly it was transforming into a power center of its own, breeding leadership, publications, protest, organization, even political influence upon the major parties. Mostly it knocked on the door of the white conscience with insistently louder and louder knocks, pointing out religious, historical and spiritual contradiction.

Among many Negroes a consequence of seeing the separate and prejudicial nature of the white church was to produce a breakaway from the black church and to project a hunt for other solutions to spiritual-material problems. In the 1930s there would rise cults based upon communal sharing of depression poverty. Evangelical cults developed. Islam appeared among the Negroes. One famous Negro preacher went to Congress and, propelled and sustained by his church, stayed there. In the South masses of Negroes, given to belief in prayer and the power of the Testaments, in faith that the Christian creed of sharing—might one day become a reality for them sought in Christian nonviolence technique a path to material salvation.

It was out of this tradition that the Negro as Bible student developed, and it is not remarkable that in the recently developed civil rights movement, the churchmen of Alabama should play so decisive a role and discover how to harness the concepts of Christianity to the needs of a liberating advance.

If it appears to observers or outsiders that the Negro in America today is a religious figure, devoted to church and to exploration into spiritual ideologies, if he experiments even with the invention of religions, gods, in his own midst, it should be recalled that it is a consequence of what has been done to him and what avenues were left open to him and to his own inventive genius.

Finding some solace in the church, educating themselves and developing leaders in this structure, relying on Negro pastors to represent them in trying to secure the ear of Federal leaders, the Negro people did the best they could inside a totally caged and crated condition.

By 1910 and 1912 the waves of the political heat of

Europe were reaching our shores. With the advent of World War I in 1914, interest in the international scene tended to further deflate the effect of black protest. The Negroes were beginning to build their own economy, to enter the insurance business because white companies would not insure them; to print weekly newspapers of protest and community interest because the white press ignored them or mis-portrayed them; to acquire property when that was possible. A Negro middle class began making an appearance—but this class was as segregated in its living habits and the attitudes toward it as the black farmer, miner or factory worker.

The new President, Woodrow Wilson, was to preside in the period when Negro respect, dignity and worth seemed to be at its lowest phase.

Wilson, who lived through the Reconstruction period and wrote about that time in tones of fear of black advance, was during two administrations cool to and silent about the Afro-American. In that epoch the Negro was at the nadir of his condition.

Born in the South, presiding over Princeton University for eight years at a time when that institution excluded Negroes, Wilson was rated as one of the world's great democrats because at the end of World War I he proposed the League of Nations.

Before his first election to the Presidency he promised Bishop Alexander Walters of the African Methodist Episcopal Zion Church that he wished to see justice done to the colored in every matter and justice executed with liberality and cordiality. "I want to assure them that should I become President of the United States they may count upon me for absolute fair dealing, for everything by which I could assist in advancing their race in the United States."

This assurance caused Dr. W. E. B. DuBois, then

leader of the National Association for the Advancement of Colored People, to support Wilson in the 1912 elections, even though he had no hearty conviction that in Wilson was there a lurking Lincoln.

Wilson's administrations from 1912 through 1920 occurred at a time when the status of the Afro-American was seemingly stationary, frozen, looking as immutable as Southern supremacist exponents claimed it was and was supposed to be.

As Wilson prepared to go to war for democracy against Germany and its allies, the state governments in the South and throughout the West enacted extensive anti-Negro legislation. Neither Wilson nor Congress opposed such "states rights" legislation.

The Negro entered the armed forces as a Jim Crow soldier in separate services. He was shipped out to the war fronts speedily when he resented segregation practices; and he was exclusively employed in the engineer or hard labor corps.

While the Negro fought in a war ostensibly and actually for the preservation of democracy, he preserved at the same time his own caste status in the armed forces and within the American milieu.

When black troops returned to the United States the traditional postwar democratic massacres awaited them and their people.

Disappointed in their country, they listened keenly when a new voice, Marcus Garvey, arrived from Jamaica and told them that life in the United States for them was hopeless and he urged their return to Africa.

Garvey touched the depth of the Afro-American's isolation.

The policy of colonization, which had no popularity when Lincoln enunciated it during the Civil War, now seemed to millions of submerged blacks as perhaps a necessity. The long bridge from the emancipation period through to the 1920s when the Negro was only a line or two above chattel slavery and in a subdued, frozen caste status was junctured only when Marcus Garvey tapped the emotional turmoil of several millions who by now despaired of the United States and were serious about returning to Africa.

The Marcus Garvey period represented the peak of white American mistreatment of Afro-Americans. By that time the displacement of the black seemed so total as to be hopeless. It must have been so or Garvey would not have captured the imagination of what has been estimated as half the Negro population.

White America had finished reshaping the American Negro into a psychological end-product. The wave of black nationalism which swept the Negro in the post World War I period had been produced by all the prior ages, stages and phases of subjugation. It had made one wing of Afro-Americans so deeply sensitive about themselves and their relation to the American scene that they now called themselves or were called by others Black Nationalists.

This phenomenon—though the Garvey program was not fulfilled—was to remain permanent in the psyche of the black man and it has led to the policies of the present period when the Negro nationalist often opposes the integrationist in the search for liberation and equal rights.

About two years before the Civil War Charles Darwin's theory of evolution had exploded upon a startled world. Ideas of evolution had been in the air for many years. But Darwin's work was a full-dressed documented theory of evolution "by means of natural selection, or the

preservation of favored races in the struggle of life."
Darwin used the term "races" as meaning all biological
matter, everything which bred. But another Englishman,
the philosopher Herbert Spencer, who had also been writing about evolution since 1852, interpreting Darwin, hit
on the theory that evolution could be applied to all sci-
ences. Evolution might explain not only the workings in
biology but also the way social and political history developed, even the way planets revolved around suns. In
his essay on *The Theory of Population* he coined the
expressions "struggle for existence" and "survival of the
fittest." Spencer applied these ideas to the social scene, to
politics, to contemporary history and to the struggle between classes. His outlook carried him into one conservative position after another: voting wasn't necessary,
women shouldn't secure the franchise, the rich should be
allowed to aggrandise their fortunes for their wealth pictured their "fitness," and labor unions and strikes were
no help to the worker. One of Spencer's American disci-
ples was Andrew Carnegie who claimed that after he
read Spencer he saw the light, beheld the truth of evolution.

Spencer's influence spread in this country through the
period of the Reconstruction. His philosophy pleased the
new Northern industrialists who considered themselves
to be "the fittest." Senator George Hearst, father of William Randolph Hearst, described members of the United
States Senate as "the fittest." Businessmen, wishing no
restriction upon the building of trusts and the making of
alliances with other "fittest" powers in Europe, took inspiration from the Spencerian theory. In practice they
interpreted the theory to mean—anything goes.

Such a rationale of unobstructed power was perfect for
a nation towering over the prostrate Afro-American. The
Caucasian was the fittest, of course. The black man, as

everyone knew, was less fit and his condition proved it. Darwin's theory of evolution implied it, they thought; and Spencer's ideas backed Darwin.

The role of words is important in the history of man's misunderstanding of man. Words, terms, slogans have disrupted societies. Around the time when "Caucasian" power was so ferociously projected, Thomas Huxley, an interpreter and supporter of Darwin, had something to say about the origin of the expression "Caucasian race." In his essay, *Man's Place in Nature,* he wrote: "Of all the odd myths that have arisen in the scientific world, the 'Caucasian mystery' invented quite innocently by Johann Blumenbach is the oddest. A Georgian woman's skull was the handsomest in his collection. Hence it became his model exemplar of human skulls from which all others might be regarded as deviations; and out of this by some strange intellectual hocus-pocus grew up the notion that the Caucasian man is the proto-typic 'Adamic' man and his country the primitive centre of our kind."

For Northern and Southern white supremists, Herbert Spencer was a godsend for their purposes. In magazines and press the term "survival of the fittest" went into general use and the inevitable deduction made by the white populace was that the black was not as "fit" as the white. The new intellectual sanction became the latest in the long series of forces laid upon the man from Africa. Small bigoted minds of the day derived new strength from misapplication of Darwin and literal application of Spencer. Pseudo-scientific notions about national and racial relations developed: essayists, novelists, economic observers used the new philosophy and biology to secure and protect the gains of class and caste. This movement combined the old taxonomic method of classifying and grading "races" with the new sociological interpretations of

Spencer; the whole development became known as Social Darwinism.

Supremacist philosophy and practice was already a century old, but it consolidated and became more turgid after the addition of Spencerian refinements. Darwin's theory had delivered blows to religious thinking, so the racists, to shore up their status at a time when they could no longer secure comfort or backing from religious or Christian tradition, hailed "the new science" as supporting their superman claims.

In this milieu an English figure of much prominence, Charles Wentworth Dilke, appeared on stage to project a mythical world of a reviving "Saxondom": whites to rule the world, with the English-speaking elements predominant.

As a younger man, not yet in the British Parliament, Dilke had come to America at the close of the Civil War to study postwar conditions. He was enamored of all English-descended peoples, whether Northern or Southern. To Dilke the Rebels and the Union men were both white and Anglo-Saxon; he would have supported the victory of either. Since the Northern cause prevailed, Dilke remarked that the ultimate future of any one section of the English race was of little moment apart from its triumph as a whole. In 1869 his *Greater Britain* was published in the United States and England and the term "Greater Britain," like the clause "survival of the fittest," spread rapidly among the English in the English dominions, and repeated even in the United States by many Americans who were described by Dilke as "American Anglomaniacs." These Americans who sought reunification with Mother England loved all things English; they were the white of the white; and Dilke took the position that all things which could be done in practical politics to reunite these elements separated by an ocean, a century and a revolution, should now be done. But passing beyond mere reunion of the United States with old England, he said that the power of English laws and English principles of government was not merely an English question; its continuance was essential to the freedom of mankind.

In succeeding years he became Sir Charles Wentworth Dilke, member of England's House of Parliament, and wrote further racist books, such as *The Present Positions of European Politics* and *Problems of Greater Britain.* The latter was published in 1890, when British imperialism was the power of the world. Dilke, one of its greatest exponents, now looked with pride upon numerous developments of policy which confirmed his efforts and his view that American-English reunification was in course.

Dilke was delighted with what he saw around him. "Already in America," he wrote, "and in Canada and Australia, there is, except as regards the treatment of the negroes and the Chinese, a deep respect for the laws which all have helped to make . . . already there is a manly give-and-take between different classes, combining respect for superiority of any kind with a total absence of servility; and there is discernible neither a tendency to anarchy on the one side nor, as between white man and white man, a tendency to oppression."

Dilke observed restoration of Southern Democrat rule and he noted that everything was being done that could be done so the two races should never meet. He had talked with Southerners, he said, and they had told him that if the race instinct did not exist it would be necessary to invent it as "the pledge of the integrity of each race, and of peace between the races." The Southerners by now believed that they were acting upon a "race instinct" and they didn't realize that they had really invented race a long time ago and they were still generating it.

Race was so much a part of their environment and mind by now that the Southerners in all honesty thought that it was right and natural and had always existed.

As the Teutonism and anti-Africanism of Dilke coalesced with the racism so high in America, there was a forecast of Twentieth Century repercussions. Germany was listening and taking delight in the way one Englishman and American after another placed Germany high in the Teutonic order. By the latter part of the century West Coast newspapers raised the howl of a "yellow peril"—a term and a fear that became national.

A belt of Anglo-Nordic-Teutonic figures bridged America with England and Germany; they all seemed to be working on a tri-racial political competition of yellows, blacks and whites. The "true" Caucasians even resented the olive-complected whites of Southern Europe. On the Continent the work of Count de Gobineau was revived and Gobineau societies spread. They had introduced into world politics an ingredient differing from nationalism. They had erected racialism to the level of a diplomatic value. Dilke, by now regarded as an architect of English imperialism, had an audience of "elite" in the United States, and what he was saying was being echoed in the highest places.

In the United States Senate men like Albert T. Beveridge and Henry Cabot Lodge expressed the elite's right to rule through being naturally superior. President Theodore Roosevelt was infected with this outlook. A Yale professor, William Graham Sumner, wrote articles for serious journals in which he equated the old-fashioned racial superiority classifications of the taxonomists with the "survival of the fittest" techniques that had emerged from Spencer's interpretation of evolution.

A widely read historian, John Fiske, who revised and extended the old Manifest Destiny idea, perceived American destiny as an alliance with Mother England and with the old Nordic-Teutonic elements of Europe. All this was an active anti-black, anti-Africa outlook. It had the effect of piling up inside the white psyche, imbedding "Caucasian"-consciousness ever deeper upon the public mind.

These men sounded more or less alike, their language arrogant and piercing. Such was Senator Beveridge's pronouncement in the United States Senate on January 9th, 1900, when Hitler was eleven years old: "We will not renounce our part in the mission of our race, trustee under God, of the civilization of the world . . . He has marked us as His chosen people to lead in the regeneration of the world . . . The question is elemental. It is racial. God has not been preparing the English-speaking and Teutonic people for a thousand years for nothing but vain and idle contemplation and self-administration. No! He has made us master organizers of the world."

Four countries participated in the development of "Caucasian"-racist ideology: the United States first and foremost in its practice, England in its theory and philosophy, France which was always mercurial, filled with heretics, proud and chauvinistic men, and Germany which lay in wait as the intellectual and physical Satan of the racist plan.

It took another Englishman, an eloquent, literary and venomous "philosopher," to synthesize the several centuries of experience and thinking and hand it on a silver-white platter to Adolf Hitler.

In the 1890s English-born Houston Stewart Chamberlain, son of an admiral and subsequent son-in-law of composer Richard Wagner, was working on a two-volume book called *Foundations of the Nineteenth Century* which was to exert important effect on Hitler twenty-five years later. His book espoused a racial theory which consummated and crystallised all prior racial writing. It stemmed in large part from the earlier work of Count de Gobineau; it utilized the classification approaches which belonged to the early offshoots of Linnaeus, and finally cited the "survival of the fittest" abortions of Spencer. What was most interesting about his work was that he drew so much of his inspiration, as had de Gobineau before him, from the American experience of keeping the black soul in America submerged.

Chamberlain, an Anglo-Saxon thinker like Dilke but with strong pro-German overtones, evolved a theory of anti-Semitism which Hitler would make programmatic. In Europe, where there were few blacks, there was a historical concern with the Jews. Chamberlain made this group his main target, but like Hitler later, he had little praise for any others in the world if they weren't Teutons.

He spoke the same language as John Fiske in America and Dilke in England when he said to the Germans: "We Teutons have certainly in the course of time developed into national individualities marked by absolutely distinct characteristics; moreover, we are surrounded by various half-brothers, but we form a unity of such strong coherence, each part of which is so absolutely essential to the other, that even the political development of the one country exercises an influence on all the others and is in turn influenced by them, but its civilization and culture can in no way be described as something isolated and autonomous."

He described the spread of the Anglo-Saxon over the world as the most important phenomenon in modern politics. He was proudest of all of the English conquest of the American colonies. He beheld in the white racial imprint all his future dreams for the spread of Twentieth Century supremacy.

All racial theorists, even Chamberlain, have their special leaning and fetishes. Chamberlain disliked the darker-skinned but still predominantly white people of Southern Europe; he wasn't at all sure they were part of the Caucasian world. He felt that the people of the Levant had become Africanized. There had been a great interbreeding in Southern Europe and he referred to these interbred populations as "half-breed souls of degenerate Southern Europe." Color was the line of demarcation, the determinant in his description of the Germans as "the fittest." He said that in India too it was *"varna,"* color which distinguished the white conquering Aryan from the defeated black man, the *Dasyu.* He referred to the peoples around the Mediterranean as the "Chaos," because they were infiltrated with Africa. Like Hitler later he attacked nearly every one in the world except the peoples in that Teutonic strip which ran from Northern Europe into North America.

Like Dilke, Chamberlain regarded the American colonies and later the United States of America as the peculiar and particular accomplishment of his own country and countrymen. Transplanted Englishman, all Teuton in blood and vigor, gave the world its greatest example of how powerful and fit the white man was and how and why the world must look to the Nordic-Teuton as the hope of the future. To understand what the Germans must do in Europe, we should look to what the English-moved-to-America had done to the Indians and the Negroes.

How the American Indian was vanquished demonstrated the forthright capacities for extermination to be found in the bold surviving white man. "We are thrilled with horror when we read the history of the annihilation of the Indians in North America," he said. "Everywhere on the side of the Europeans there is injustice, treachery, savage cruelty; and yet how decisive was this very work of destruction for the later development of a noble thoroughly Teutonic nation upon that soil!"

Chamberlain was pleased with the similarity of his viewpoint with that of the Briton-descended, Teuton-minded Fiske. Fiske's *Destiny of Man* was a Social Darwinian book. In Fiske's interpretation, "the struggle for existence had succeeded in bringing forth that consummate product of creative activity, the human soul . . ." Fiske had also said that it was the wholesale destruction of life, which had heretofore characterised evolution ever since life began, through which the higher forms of organic existence had been produced.

Chamberlain's method, in order to discredit a whole people, a church, an institution, even a whole continent, was to show that it had been "tainted" with the African influence. He swept away South American culture as mongrel, beheld the Christian Church as contaminated by the "refuse of humanity from Africa, Egypt and elsewhere." After relying upon ethnologists who had decried blacks in the United States, South America and in Africa, he returned to the wondrous works of his Teuton relatives in the United States. Here was Britain's own culture all over again and in a new high stage of development. The grand example was that of the French and English in the United States—exterminating, exterminating, and enslaving. "No one can prove that the predominance of Teutonism is a fortunate thing for all the inhabitants of the earth; from the earliest times down to today we see the Teutons, to make room for themselves, slaughtering whole tribes and races, or slowly killing them by systematic demoralization. That the Teutons with their virtues alone and without their vices—such as greed, cruelty, treachery, disregard of all rights but their own right to rule etc.—would have won the victory, no one will have the audacity to assert, but every one must admit that in the very places they were most cruel—as, for instance, the Anglo-Saxons in England, the German Order in Prussia, the French and English in North America—they laid by this very means the surest foundation of what is highest and most moral."

England was making ready for an imperial leap upon Africa; so were other European countries. This was a revived extension of the old political concept: cheap labor based upon pigmentation, upon the accessibility of the African and his incapacity for self-defense by modern military means.

Impressed by the example of the American success, the European nations, in the latter part of the previous century, contemplated the imperial sacking of Africa. Convinced that America had grown in power by its extermination of the Indian and its reincasement of the Negro in a new land of serfdom, several European countries descended upon Africa again.

By now, they decided, they too could work with the fully rounded out, "scientifically" rationalized Linnaeus-Darwin-Spencer-derived concept of black inferiority.

Four centuries of racism in America had helped breed a new way of political thinking. Pigment and physiology entered politics everywhere.

The principle of race, which see-sawed back and forth from England to the American colonies, and back to Europe in our post-Civil War period, with Dilke, Chamberlain and others acting as transmission agents, became consummate with the development of the Third Reich. Although our country gave important concepts of liberty and democracy to the world, Hitler and his supporters finally snatched from modern American-African-European history the root of racialism and replanted it for our bloody time. It is not a far cry, only a loud one, from the curious anti-Africanism of John Locke to the racists of Europe who took what we had built and "improved" upon it in Europe from 1932 to 1945. The evil genie of the Third Reich sprang hydra-headed from the Amero-European lamp. Chamberlain was to become the close friend of Hitler, and Hitler later acknowledged his debt to the Englishman.

Nowhere else but in the United States was the practical pattern perfected. Despite the pool of racism in historical Germany itself, the American experience strengthened the race ideas of English, French and German white-myth seekers. The American success offered prestige, birthright and impulse for European emulation. There was no other country the Nazis could turn to and study that could yield the working method any better. As Rudolph Hess told the *New York Times* correspondent, Harold Callender, in August of 1940, "We are very much like the Ku Klux Klan." In 1936, a prominent German professor of jurisprudence, Dr. Henrich Krieger, wrote a book published in Berlin in which he examined the law, the tradition, the jurisprudence of American Jimcrow. Its title was *Das Rassenrecht in den Veringigten Staaten*. Our system of racial legality became the model for Adolf Hitler's regime. As the Southerner, W. S. Cash, put it: "In its essence the thing [white supremacy] was an authentic folk movement—at least as fully such as the Nazi movement in Germany, to which it was not without kinship."

Color and Democracy, by the late Dr. W. E. B. DuBois, published in 1945 while the war against the Third Reich was on, pointed to Hitlerian practice as originating on our soil. "The Negro problem forces the United States to abdicate its natural leadership of democracy in the world and to acquiesce in a domination of organized wealth which exceeds anything elsewhere in the world. It gives rein and legal recognition to race hate, which the Nazis copied in their campaign against the Jews, *establishing it on American lines* of caste conditions, disfranchisement, mob murder, ridicule and public disparagement."

Out of the New World and all of its wonders and beauties had come in crystal clear form one etiological fact: the racist idea. As evil is a cholera of its own, racism became, when replanted in Europe and adapted to European conditions, a wild growth destined to ravage the whole Continent. The American experience led to its logical conclusion. The historical ties between America and England and "Nordic" Europe—Fiske, Dilke, Chamberlain, and all the others on both continents together with the living example of "successful" America split down its black-white middle—showed Hitler that he too could invent a world concept of over-races and under-races.

Out of slavery and caste in America, out of the imperial invasion of Africa late in the last century and into the present came Hitler's *Mein Kampf;* and although his main target was the Jew, he spared nobody: not the Oriental, not the American, not the English. France was the eternal and the mortal enemy. The Russian was a great barbarian. And so on through most of the peoples of the world.

Yet it was the way in which Hitler referred to the blacks and to Africa that contained his surpassing slander. Out of all that had happened since the Portuguese entry into Africa and out of the guidance Hitler had received from de Gobineau and Chamberlain and the army of others who for two centuries had given wings

to the word and the concept of race, came his special
delineation which outpaced those of his progenitors. His
root feeling was antiblack, his outpourings were the
apogee after four centuries of the foundations and development of white supremacy in the United States and the
Western World.

And ultimately most of the world, including the para-
doxically racist yet democratic United States of America,
was compelled to array itself against his tyrannous stab
for world domination over all races and nations. When
Hitler moved and operated with the Aryan concept
which he and others, including Americans, had helped to
fashion, the fallacy of race lay naked, wholly exposed, a
bloody, insane, evil thing. The lordly Nordic whites
moved against other lordly whites: against their English
half-brothers socalled, against the French, the Polish, the
Danes, the Americans, the Jews, the Czechs, and finally
against the white nations inside the Soviet framework.

And, adding to the bizarre absurdities, the racially
pure Teutonic Aryans of the North had as their loyal
allies a nation of yellow-skinned armies out of the East.

Even Hitler knew the nature of the centuries-old lie,
for he told Hermann Rauschning: "I know perfectly well
that in the scientific sense there is no such thing as race
. . . I as a politician need a conception which enables the
order which has hitherto existed on historic bases to be
abolished and an entirely new and anti-historic order enforced and given an intellectual basis . . . And for this
purpose the conception of race serves me well . . ."

Often when nationalism tries to exert its claimed right
and prerogatives it draws on the raciality of spheres of
influence. Retention of this pool of moral-emotional-

scientific fallacy amounts to the livest, most universal disease in existence.

Science and serious social observation have corrected some of the myths or eliminated fallacy: but the public mind still deals with the race concept and the racial approach. The race concept resides in tribal-national mores around the world; it is more deadly than many dangerous viruses that can be seen with the electron microscope. The racial menace, now with its finger close to the nuclear button, remains a most threatening malaise of modern man.

As the Twentieth Century dawned on the modern world, the shifting, uncertain winds of racism and prejudice twisted across the American scene.

The reunion of North and South, together with the development of new ideologies and techniques of racial domination, plus the driving trend of American economy toward higher and higher frequencies of economic power by now produced a pathology in the white mind. By 1905 this land was sick to its core, sick with a sickness which was to plague the country into the present.

The South had a way of its own of symbolizing the abandonment of all pretense about the Christian-human way. The live and heavily breathing Ku Klux Klan made a mockery of the church of which it was a part. The denial of the Negro was anti-Christ, and almost without thinking, the Klan knew how to celebrate the new witchcraft.

All through the new century Christ's cross would burn —on hills, in front of black churches, on lonely roads where Afro-Americans were silenced. The burning cross became the unconscious or conscious symbol of the South's invasion of its own soul. There was nothing left

to do but crucify the blacks and burn the cross on which
Christ had died. Neither the time of Rome, nor the time
of Jerusalem, nor the medieval age of witches had seen a
more picturesque regurgitation of guilt.

Now when the cross burned it was in celebration of
five centuries of a crypto-religious invention. It celebrated the special science of American racism North and
South, and all that had gone into its making: whips,
white robes, electric prods, books, teachers, laws, slaveships, fences, Jim Crow signs, black codes, race theories,
nightsticks, slurring advertisements, supremacist parades,
money, courts, jails, sheriffs, troopers, vigilantes, flog-
gings, lynchings, separate accommodations, inadequate
segregated schools, stealing prisoners out of jails, all-
white juries, poll tax, unfair sharecropping, peonage,
Jim Crow unions, hound dogs, guns, church-burnings,
stake-burnings, third degree torture in cells, gasoline,
kerosene, matches, torches, knives, bullwhips, sale of
parts of lynched and cut up victims, Government indifference, Federal opposition, lukewarm Republicans,
church sanction, auction blocks, false witness, pine trees,
persimmon trees, terms like boy, Uncle, darky, nigger,
ape, "death at the hands of parties unknown," compromise in politics, demagogy, promises, lies, double-
lynchings, triple-lynchings, trial by mock court, newspaper offensives, rumor, gossip, slander, cayenne pepper,
circumstantial evidence, extorted confessions, Constitutional compromise, unimplemented Supreme Court decisions, tar, feathers, oil, plow lines, an indifferent
supremacist-based FBI, all-white Legislatures, false iden-
tifications, telescopic sights, chains, rum, baubles, ships,
factors, British imperial power, Portuguese profits, trade,
credit, commissions, insurance of slavetrading sloops,
handcuffs, shackles, gunpowder, swivel guns, diet of grits
and fatback, cutlasses, fevers, banks, competitive white

labor, states rights, whipping posts, hue and cry papers,
pass papers, church wardens, proclamations, curfews,
rewards for runaways, illegal search and seizure, fines,
slavecatchers, ducking, branding, dismemberment, official sadism, baptism plus slavery, cat-o-nine tails, pillory,
thirty-nine lashes, castration, divine right, a hot iron to
the body, inadmissible Negro testimony, screwing of the
hands in a vise, switches, kicking, stomping, cow hides,
cotton gin, psuedo-scientists, ambitious publicists, poor
white egos, rich white egos, self-justification, backroom
politics, filibusters, Negrophobia, conformity of white,
intolerance of political deviation, fallacious race theories, fallacious anthropology, professional race-minded
politicians, quotations from the Bible upholding master-
serf relationships, prayers for the success of slavebuying
and selling, God, Christ, Deity, the Infant, iron pipes,
machine guns, mobs, posses, avid reporters, White Citizens Councils, brass knuckles, gallows, "teaching the
niggers a lesson," false history teaching, partial history
teaching, half-truths, white supremacist coroners, the fes-
tival spirit, rubber hose, official regrets, official con-
donement, sermons by pastors calling for lynchings,
"Therefore put away from among ourselves that wicked
person" (Corinthians), conscience, turning away the
eyes, kicking it under the rug, bricks, rocks, gas bombs,
photographers, weak marshals, obscenities, curses, intim-
idation of voters, parliamentary trickery, violation of the
Fourteenth Amendment, "qualifications," legal subter-
fuges, disfranchisement, complex legal verbiage, commissions to study Negro-white relations, separate railway
car laws, Jim Crow street car laws, back of the bus, extra-
dition, chain gangs, restrictive covenant, separate toilets,
separate drinking fountains, separate cemeteries, separate motels, separate souls, racial purity campaigns, separation of black and white in theatres, public halls,

stadiums, lilywhite Democratic primary, constant embarrassment, humiliation, anguish, trembling, the Old Rugged Cross, "Servants, be obedient unto them that according to the flesh, are your masters . . ." (Ephesians), splits in churches North and South . . .

Out of all this, with the energies of millions of people engaged in the working-upon process,—out of this could come a statement by a white Virginia Baptist editor on why white Baptists could not enter into interchange of correspondence with black Baptists: "God has made the two races widely different; not only in complexion but in their instincts and social qualities. We take it for granted that it was not the purpose of the Creator that they should be blended. Nature abhors the union . . ."

But the Creator was not God in this instance; it was American history and the exigencies of American politics and economics. The whole dichotomy was born of guns and clubs and profits and church and laws, the omission of Jefferson's passage about slaves from the Declaration of Independence, the witchcraft tradition which enclosed the colonial mind further upon its pure white self, the sale of Indian men and women into servitude, the Treaty of Utrecht, sophistry of the intellectuals, the theologians and the Legislatures, the slavetrading origins of Peter Faneuil prior to the origins of Faneuil Hall, the London merchants, the West Indies nursery of American slavery, sugar, tobacco, rice, indigo, peanuts, the Fugitive Slave Act, American invention of a word like miscegenation, laws against intermarriage, unwritten right of white male access to black female, defensive nature of "the rape complex," myths about black sexuality, myths about results of black-white mixture, anti-race mixing laws in two-thirds of the states, murder of blacks for looking at white women, absentee plantation owners, brutal overseers, and this: "Good feeling between master and slave was brought about by the happy disposition and easy temperament of the slave. The black was rarely surly and dis-contented and he harbored no grudge against master for keeping him in slavery."

No grudge . . . except that resistance resulting in the Brownsville, Texas massacre; the Atlanta, Georgia, massacre; Springfield, Ohio, massacre; Springfield, Illinois, massacre; Vicksburg, Mississippi, massacre, Greenburg, Indiana, massacre . . .

Early in the present century, elements in the Federal Government, egged on by several generations of racist momentum and convinced that "race" was so real that all nations of Europe were really specific races, decided to spend three million dollars in the preparation of a *Dictionary of Races*. In 1907 nearly three hundred researchists worked for three years examining the Europeans who had entered the United States in the immigration waves of the 1880s and 1890s.

When the results were published and when every ex-national of Europe was referred to as a race—Italian, Russian, Bulgarian, Irishman, Turk, Serbo-Croatian, Pole, Greek, and so on—the interpreters of the work reached the conclusion that the recent arrivals were not as good material for American citizenship as Teutonic and Celtic stock from Western and Northern Europe. There were therefore set up immigration quotas and a limit on the number of persons entering from Lower Europe and other portions of the world.

This new period of immigration restriction uniquely crystallised a prediction made by Abraham Lincoln in correspondence with Joshua Speed before the Civil War when Lincoln expressed opposition to the Know-Nothing

policy of bigotry. He saw that the national policy of pro-
longing and extending black slavery could easily spread
to the containment of other elements. He wrote: "How
can anyone who abhors the oppression of Negroes be in
favor of degrading classes of white people? Our progress
in degeneracy appears to me to be pretty rapid. As a
nation we began by declaring that 'all men are created
equal.' We now practically read it, 'all men are created
equal except Negroes and foreigners and Catholics."

What he feared was possible actually took form in the
early 1900s. From that time until currently a new conflict, a national competition within the so-called Caucasian framework led to quota limitations upon migration
and to intergroup hostilities of a highly emotional nature.
We entered into an epoch of naked, quota-system
bigotry: to the burdened, the oppressed of the "wrong"
racial strain, the American front door was locked.

All of this stemmed from the centuries of supremacist
instillation in the American mind. The systemic barrage
revived and enforced ancient distrust, suspicion and ri-
valries. These attitudes, issuing from the top, swiftly
spread over the citizenry so that the nation by the 1920s
had a whole new collection of prejudices and Old World
bitternesses.

The *Dictionary of Races* and its mass of contorted
theory, found its embodiment in a reviving Ku Klux
Klan. In the 1920s the Klan claimed a membership of
four million and it received official permission to parade
in Washington, D.C. past the White House. Yet in this
stage it contained a seed of dissolution, for it enlarged its
purview of hatreds to include Catholics, Jews, Orientals,
immigrants and political heretics. Having moved beyond
so-called African inferiority and included so many other
peoples of alleged inferiority, the Klan revival drew a
powerful reply from many democratic thinkers, observers

and critics. Inside these opposing theoretical camps and in the organizational life of the harassed "minorities," vociferous and outraged Americans took up the challenge. Partisans lined up on opposite sides with books, lectures, newspaper propaganda and sponsorship of legislative proposals.

One of the early pioneers in the anthropoligical answer to the racist school was Franz Boas who influenced many students to participate in scientific examination of these simmering war-breeding concepts. After him others plunged into this sea of conflict, emerging with startling scientific refutations of the racist theories.

New observers made clear that variations of the human face and form had no significance where rights, brains, character, sensibilities or cultural potential or human value were concerned. Through biologists we discovered that no group of people is more advanced than any other group, for all have spent exactly the same amount of time evolving. The unity of man, they demonstrated, was a consequence of the fact that the human race has always been a single unit, that there is a common gene pool for the entire human race; that men and women of all so-called races have had children together; that there are no pure races; and that even if peoples had been reproductively isolated for thousands of years, which is not the case, the main evolution, in recent times, has been cultural.

But by now the prejudices of millions of Americans, especially in rural areas, were cherished like the family album. As of old the main gush had emanated from the South: this remained the most stubborn, unchanging part of the American mind.

While the "Caucasians" warred among themselves over the migrants from the Levant, from Southern Europe and Eastern Europe, the Afro-American remained in that relative position of struggling prostration which characterised his station from 1900 to 1929. He was regarded as being safely off to the side, secure in his segregated and educationally second-rate private colleges. The black woman was powerless, a working washwoman mother away from her family much of the time; the Negro home was often a broken home; rich and poor Negro alike were under control; the humiliation was uniform. As a result the Federal Government settled down to what it conceived to be a satisfactory legal contest with the Negro. He could get his case into the courts, the courts could and would procrastinate forever; for years this holding delaying action went on. A seemingly strangled black community permitted the white community to pursue its objectives against other competing national minorities whose presence was regarded as a threat. With the black man safely sidetracked, as in the kitchen, the basement, the elevator, the field, it mattered not if a rebellious figure like Marcus Garvey appeared. Such men could be arrested, jailed, deported, and their movement restricted or crushed. And as this occurred the power structure moved to curtail not only the Afro-American but the alleged inferior kin of the "Chaos."

In the 1920s and 1930s the Negro watched in amazement the strange racial conflicts which split the "Caucasian" community. He had no objection to limitation of migration from Europe. The Europeans, of whatever national origin, arrived with more rights at once than the black ever had. The new whites from the beginning fell into the general pattern of "Caucasian"-race thinking. The immigrant did not become a "minority" ally of the black; he arrived as a labor competitor. He also wanted to assimilate, to merge with the native white Americans and secure citizenship. Or he became nationalist and sought to preserve Old World identity and culture as a means of adding something to America. The whole "minority" sphere bore a close relationship to developing labor movement activities. These national groups in the 1930s marched as entities in labor and nationalist parades and in the parades of the American holidays. They sometimes voted in blocs, their vote being sought by politicians and parties; mostly they headed toward all-white assimilation, afraid to identify with so oppressed a group as the Afro-American.

So, in the period of quotas, the Negro in politics offered no objections except to restrictions against migration of colored West Indians. It is probable that the Afro-American gained political strength out of that limitation upon migration which developed sharply in 1931 and held in force through 1945.

During this time Hitler had taken over and altered the racial eddies generating on two continents, launching Teutonic-war against the European "Chaos"—which now included Saxon England—and he found himself swiftly arrayed against color-national-racial-political elements of most of Europe and America. In this same period, with World War II on, Mary McLeod Bethune, the Negro educator, urged young Negroes to look beyond their subjective colored selves and to identify with a suffering internationality of peoples. "Lift your eyes from your puddle of discontent and look about you at the angry sea of human misery and suffering throughout the world," she said. "Learn to think first as Americans and secondly as Negroes—but always as alert, humane, broadly intelligent members of the human race."

By now the Afro-American had been so battered by the supremacist hammer that he had often become an anvil-like product. He was neither an American nor a citizen of the world; he was an enraged and subjective "colored" figure bewildered by his outnumbering, by being trapped, and by uncertainty as to whether or not there was any solution anywhere. Yet he was engaged in a multi-sided quest for directions, solutions, answers. What he had to work with now was mostly a collective rage not yet wholly known to himself, not known at all to the church-going, prayer-murmuring power structures in the United States.

From the 1932 election of Franklin D. Roosevelt to the Presidency, through the early 1960s, comprehensive changes occurred in the total national scene. Industrial and economic transformation took place, a great war occurred, the nation became increasingly urbanized, there were migrations of Negroes into Northern cities. The Afro-American, aided by shifting policies at high governmental levels and alternating currents in major and minor parties, jimmied himself into a position where by 1940 his vote became decisive in ten Northern states. The Negro had quite thoroughly shifted his allegiance from the Republican Party to the Democratic Party after the Presidency of Herbert Hoover. When, among Roosevelt's earliest moves there was the declaration that the South was Economic Problem No. 1, a share of Federal assistance reached the Negroes. On lower levels new organizations entered the field to assist the black in labor and income directions. These developments, along with the existence of various civil liberties cases which aroused the attention of the country, tended to break the old entrenched ideas.

The war against the Nazis focused attention upon the domestic contradiction. The Negroes pointed to the comparability of the United States pattern with that which Hitler proclaimed and sought to execute. Riots in Harlem revealed the growing Negro discontent with the traditional conditions while being called upon to support the war against European fascism. Early in the course of the conflict President Roosevelt faced the same problem as that which had confronted George Washington and Abraham Lincoln. As they had moved from military necessity to include Negroes in their specific causes, now the New Deal President had to respond to huge pressures demanding that he remove discriminatory policies in defense production. Not until A. Philip Randolph, the union leader, threatened an all-Negro March on Washington did the Federal Government yield and issue a policy against discrimination in employment. Comparable pressures by Negroes and their allies made inroads upon segregation policies in the armed services. Once more an old pattern was reaffirmed: the Afro-American could make some steps forward when there was foreign or national crisis. But such gains have always been hard won. In Detroit there was a massacre of Negroes. In Harlem there were riots, and in other cities vigorous protests.

When the war was over there followed the usual postwar violence and the nation North and South resumed working upon its ancient pattern of containing the returned soldier and the Negro civilian inside the old cages. This time the effort was not so successful. Postwar violence in the South drove hundreds of thousands to migrate to the North and West. In some twenty-five cities of the North huge ghettos were filling up and congesting. But in these places Negroes could vote. Large numbers, not necessarily able to find work and often living on relief, did go to the polls.

The Democrats, in 1948, became the chief beneficiaries of these political changes. During "the age of conformity"' under Truman and Eisenhower international fears beset Federal government; the liberal and radical

voice was hushed; the third party movement of Henry A.
Wallace was badly defeated; it was followed by a general
sublimation of the progressive protest. Labor itself in the
Congress of Industrial Organization and the American
Federation of Labor entered largely into conservative and
silent currents. White liberals remained generally silenced until about 1958. But none of these developments, none of the conservative domination within the
white community and inside the major parties, greatly
affected or altered the condition of the Afro-American.
He had always been submerged; his protest had been
constant before "the age of conformity" and it continued
in a plodding way throughout that period.

In the latter part of the decade, from 1955 to 1960,
the entire white labor-liberal community, still silent and
concerned in academic circles with a "rediscovery of national value" took note of intensive civil rights activity in
Southern states, notably in Alabama. The Negro American had now seized the initiative as a force in the land,
and raised itself above the general horizon of liberal protest. Its activity, presence and demand were everywhere
noted. The whites, welcoming an ally in the democratic
battle and a breakthrough in the conformist atmosphere,
came to the support of the rigorous civil rights activity led
and participated in mainly by Negroes. It was a new
phenomenon in American politics. It was the first time in
national history that the Negro himself led a militant liberal force both North and South.

The result was a resurrection of the democratic protest
tradition which, by the time John F. Kennedy became
President, was enormous, vocal, effective in every locale,
and was attracting attention everywhere in the world.

Throughout the preceeding thirty-year period there
had been little or no economic change in the general
status of the Afro-American. He had remained rigidly

inside the old caste structure. But there were ecological shifts. A majority of the Negroes were now living in the North and the West. In some ways their living condition had worsened. It was worse than ever in the congested ghettos, particularly in New York, Detroit, and Chicago. These were already old ghettos but now, their population had doubled. While there appeared to be a gain nationally in terms of activity, protest, Federal and State decisions, and the issuance of tons of rhetoric and promises by politicians and parties, there was still no appreciable alteration in the fundamental status of the Negro from what it had been in the previous generation. There were large segments of literacy in the black group, but there remained pools of illiteracy which numbered hundreds of thousands. There were thousands of middle classmen, but there were still millions of unemployed, while the employed themselves were still being paid half wages, working part time and held to menial and transitory work. An early death rate was higher among Negroes than white. The infant mortality rate among Negroes continued twice as high. Almost every social condition of a negative order occurred in double or treble measure among the Negroes.

Still the thirty-year period varied from other phases of the American past. The Negro, largely by his own efforts, moved to a new political level; he was a force, a cohesive and crowning power himself, affecting every stream of white society. The demand for civil rights legislation reached such a proportion that, in one move after another, State and Federal Government, together with the Supreme Court, acted to accord the Afro-American at least on paper—his constitutional rights.

Some of it was real, reflecting the genuine concern in the hearts and desires of millions of whites. Much of it was political gesturing, with white politicians counting on long-delayed legal actions. Yet in the decade 1956 to 1966 the Negro became the paramount social issue. A large-scale civil rights force moved to the surface of society. Its interest dominated all others, save that of a bloc trying to prevent nuclear war. Even in that area the civil rights issue merged with the international questions of war, peace and human rights.

Economic gains remained few or non-existent or token. The Negro sustained and intensified his restiveness over continued denials of his political and legal aims. Unemployment, second-rate education, ghetto living, the broken family, and segregation from the general national community seemed as petrified as ever.

But the Negro and his white allies mounted an approach that embraced every policy known to practical politics and diplomacy. While one wing pursued legal redress, another picketed for economic rights, a third took to nationalism, and a fourth conducted an effective nonviolent moralist campaign. What appeared clear was that the Afro-American had mastered such understanding of the national picture that his leaders were able to register and vote the black mass and that both leaders and followers learned to strike at every vulnerable spot in the polity. With these developments some genuine breakthroughs occurred.

Still none of this altered the rigidity of the ancient system. Moreover, a most significant development, as the civil rights thrust junctured the national economy and morality, was that the struggle moved northward. The latent large pockets of tribal mistrust and ignorance in the huge northern centers became provoked into the open. It was necessary for this to occur or the question could never be settled. Then the sullenness of the mentality of many of the white Northerners stood exposed. A century and a half earlier de Tocqueville observed that there was a more bitter hatred of the ex-African among white Northerners; now this became sadly confirmed; only it was a century and a half later, and the psyche was that much more encrusted.

The steady development of a civil rights pressure bloc, from 1910 on, when the National Association for the Advancement of Colored People was formed, was consummated in a decision of Federal Government in 1957 to establish a *United States Commission on Civil Rights*. In 1961 this Commission published five volumes dealing with Voting, Education, Employment, Housing and Justice. Added to these was a *Fifty States Report Submitted to the Committee on Civil Rights by the State Advisory Committee*. This huge picture on the condition of the Negro in America in relation to all structures of society, and primarily to Federal Government, revealed that the Federal Government itself North and South was a prime mover in violation of Negro rights. The report uniformly and unsparingly revealed the role of realtors, bankers and corporations of all kinds in maintaining the national pattern of the ghetto and the deprived black man, to the advantage of the white worker, the white middleclass and the white upperclass. Home financiers, builders, lenders, all were shown to be guilty of ignoring the Negro or denying his appeals or circumventing his approaches. Federal resources themselves aided and abetted private industry. Congress was accused of remaining silent about a majority of states which participated in maintaining discrimination in housing; Federal funds were often used in a discriminatory manner, with the Federal Government doing nothing about it.

The report, venturing into every corner of American life, examined racism in jury selections, police brutality, restrictions in great variety in the whole realm of education. It confirmed the results of the whole tradition of jim crow, bluntly charging that the State Governments, as well as the Federal Government, were deeply involved in organized racism. It relentlessly denounced white structure itself as the significant factor in maintaining black oppression.

What devolves today upon the Afro-American, and remains now his task—unless he retreats into some separatist, black nationalism—is the continuous process of winning for himself his goal of true equality out of the whole syndrome of white power, culture, prestige, wealth, together with its whole panoply of values, good and bad. The Negro must move into the national fabric with the objective, stated and unstated, of taking on the good and evil about and over him. He must be a part of it all. For the only other alternative is the separate world, the separate culture of some black nationalist revival.

The upheaval toward realization is largely on the levels of dignity, respect, amity, accord, fellowship, human right, understanding of man by man.

That is the nexus—nothing else, not even jobs, which are sometimes given; not even votes, which have been granted; not even equal accommodations, which are part of law, not even favorable Supreme Court decisions.

The final specific task is for the white citizen to undo his diabolical inventive genius, to transcend an unconscionable tradition. It is in a realm beyond legislation, even though legislation and all other political and economic steps are integral to the process. The great alterations and concessions must emerge from that side which generated the entire distorted history.

What is needed is not so much revolution as rebirth—
psychical, spiritual human recall and renovation. This
is something far beyond mere reconstruction. For the
total concept is Resurrection, finally proceeding—
the sooner the better—from death to life.

NOTE AND BIBLIOGRAPHY

Source references appear frequently throughout this book, as may have been noted. Few books by or about 'Negroes' *per se* are listed below. The premise of this interpretive account has been based primarily upon European history and "white" American history, as representing the origins of the Afro-American's condition.

In the first part there has been much reliance upon Elizabeth Donnan's *Documents Illustrative of the History of the Slave Trade to America*. This work is itself composed of primary research undertaken by Miss Donnan. There are many viewpoints which can be derived from a study of her four volumes published by the Carnegie Institution of Washington in 1930. The documents, letters and records have been studied for the picture they contain of how European traders, merchants and governments invaded Africa, opened the slave trade, transported Africans and forced them into the New World mould of slavery.

Owing to the impressive role of the Popes and the Catholic Church generally in the invasion of Africa and the spread of slavery in the West, the papal bulls of Eugenia IV, Nicholas V and Alexander VI, in the Fifteenth Century, have been examined. These documents, of course, disclose papal encouragement of the conquest of land and humans for both "soul salvation" and trade. The bulls may be read in Frances G. Davenport's *Euro-*

pean Treaties Bearing on the History of the United States (Washington, 1917). The New York Public Library has the papal documents.

Christopher Columbus, Mariner, by Samuel Eliot Morison, contains "Columbus's Letter to Santangel" written in the Canary Islands and finished on February 15th, 1493. The letter, referred to by Morison as "the first of all *Americana,*" reveals Columbus as conqueror and would-be enslaver, and is the prelude to what is now the civil rights conflict.

The single great "accomplishment" of the Western invention or recreation of the Afro-American was in the sustained effort to rob the ex-African of his humanity. An important study is Gomes Eannes de Azurara's report of Prince Henry the Navigator's invasion of the African coast. His narrative, condensed and translated, appears in the Donnan collection of slavery documents. Azurara, royal librarian and keeper of the archives of Portugal, may have been the first writer-historian to begin a picture of the African as a heathen, pagan, inferior being.

For the section *Into the New World,* with its emphasis upon how the English culture primarily saturated and submerged the ex-African, there is the enormous literature of the colonial period. Traditional historians such as Rhodes, Fiske, McMasters, Astley, and Hakluyt reveal pictures of the English cultural-religious impact upon the New World and such histories often became my "primary research" because of needed reinterpretation of their viewpoints. The works of philosopher John Locke show his pendulum swinging from liberal constitutionalism to his tolerance of slaves. Charles S. Mangum's *The Legal Status of the Negro* discloses the governmental legislative push against the ex-African, generation after generation. Contemporary historians like the late Charles A. Beard, and Allan Nevins and Henry S. Commager, were observed for their special schismatic outlook. A better way of putting it is to say that they have treated history as a white history in a white world filled with white records, archives and documents. But often, in the books of such historians, there have been brief passages, like sudden lights, which have revealed the hidden inventing process of the Afro-American.

The words of Washington, Madison, Jefferson, Hamilton and other Founding Fathers disclose how they felt about the master-slave relationship. As a rule the sources examined have been mentioned in the text; for example, such a fundamental document as Jefferson's *Notes From Virginia*. One of the best stocks for the understanding of American history, from its founding through the Civil War, is in the extensive writings of William H. Seward. Though he was primarily a public figure and statesman he was also a first-rate historian, and he probed the earliest periods of American society to illuminate his moves and the directions of society during the crucial antislavery period. He understood and portrayed the role of government and "white" society in "making" the slave. His voluminous work is gathered in a special collection at Rochester University.

The Federalist Papers indicate more about the Constitution than what appears in the document itself, notably the views of Madison, Jay and Hamilton. Since the Constitution was a major product, in effect, dooming and imprisoning the slave and the free Negro, that document and interpreters of that document required special examination.

To the sections dealing with the Civil War and Reconstruction the same special approach has been brought, the Emancipation Proclamation itself being examined with a view to what it did and did not do for the freed slave and for the light it sheds on the continuing displacement of the Afro-American. The literature on these periods is enormous and some of the books studied are noted below. Anyone examining American history books, sources, papers, pamphlets, literature and newspapers, having in mind a special outlook—in my case, that a continuous "river" of inventivity could be discovered—must of necessity range over whole stacks of material. It was possible to stand in the stacks of a library for hours and leaf through scores of books on economics, government, history and sociology, and find incessantly references, passages, bits, statements, confirming as a regular process of national life the organized and motivated force of the white oversociety in its operations against the sublimated Afro-American. As these processes go on daily in the United States, they become reflected in all literature —now as in the past. It is therefore difficult to point to any and all "sources" for the present viewpoint or to suggest that it derives only from specific information in specific books. In an earlier book, *Jim Crow America*, which this writer published in 1947, the views which are set forth in depth in *The Invention of the Negro* were then presented in preliminary form, projecting the same words and conception, namely, that the so-called Negro was an "invention," "creation," "man-made," "manufactured," "evolved," "born and nurtured out of economic greed," "Race. Made in the U.S.A.," "evolved fetishism of 'race,' " and so forth.

There is a large literature on race *per se* which returns to the time of Linnaeus. Some titles are indicated in the text of the book and other references appear in the list of books to follow.

One of the most interesting streams of writing, bearing heavily upon present-day world problems, is the racial historiography of men like Houston Stewart Chamberlain and Sir Charles W. Dilke, figures antipodal to the Afro-

American. These men and their deeds are end products of prior European history and its auxiliary national American history. They and their ideas of supremacy and imperialism evolved inevitably out of the history, writings and human experience initiated by Columbus and the monarchs of Spain and Portugal. Their works referred to late in *The Invention,* dealing with the rise and congealing of the racial concept in the times of World War II, remain unfortunately a pertinent stream of inquiry because of the current large East-West conflict and because of the persisting tribalisms and ethno-racial misunderstandings. The tendency of world statesmanship to think in terms of East and West, Orient and Occident, and other geo-ethnic divisions, only illustrates that the processes virulent for the last half millenium have spiraled into international configurations and conflicts. A few sources dealing with these outlooks and areas are also listed.

THE BOOKS

Adams, James Truslow. *America's Tragedy*. N. Y., Scribner's Sons, 1941.

Adams, James Truslow. *The Epic of America*. Boston, Little, Brown & Co., 1933.

Adams, James Truslow. *Revolutionary New England*. Boston, Atlantic Monthly Press, 1923.

Adams, *The Works of John*. (ed. C. F. Adams) Boston, 1856.

Adams, *The Writings of Samuel*. (ed. H. A. Cushing) N. Y., G. P. Putnam's Sons, 1904-08.

Andrews, Charles McLean. *The Colonial Period of American History*. New Haven, Yale University Press, 1934.

Andrews, Charles McLean. *The Colonial Background of the Revolution*. New Haven, Yale University Press, 1939.

Babcock, K. C. *The Rise of American Nationality*. N. Y., Harper & Bros., 1906.

Ballagh, J. C. *A History of Slavery in Virginia*. Baltimore, Johns Hopkins Press, 1902.

Bancroft, G. *History of the United States*. Boston, Little, Brown & Co., 1841.

Beard, Charles A. *An Economic Interpretation of the Constitution of the United States*. N. Y., Macmillan, 1960.

Beard, Charles A. and Mary T. *The Rise of American Civilization*. N. Y., Macmillan Co., 1936.

Beard, Charles A. and Mary T. *History of the United States*. N. Y., Macmillan Co., 1941.

Beer, G. L. *The Old Colonial System*. N. Y., Peter Smith, 1933.

Benedict, Ruth. *Race, Science, and Politics*. N. Y., The Viking Press, 1945.

Boas, Franz. *Race and Democratic Society*. N. Y., J. J. Augustin, 1945.

Bolton, H. E. and Marshall, T. M. *The Colonization of North America, 1492-1783*. N. Y., Macmillan Co., 1935-1937.

Bowers, Claude G. *Jefferson and Hamilton*. Boston, Houghton, Mifflin Co., 1925.

Bowers, Claude G. *The Tragic Era: The Revolution After Lincoln*. Cambridge, Houghton, Mifflin Co., 1929.

Buck, Paul H. *The Road to Reunion*. Boston, Little, Brown and Company, 1937.

Cable, George W. *The Negro Question*. Garden City, N. Y., Doubleday, 1958.

Callender, G. S. *Selections from the Economic History of the United States, 1765-1860*. Boston, N. Y., Ginn & Co., 1909.

Carnegie Institution of Washington. *Documents Illustrative of the Slave Trade to America*. Washington, D. C., Carnegie Institution, 1930-35.

Cash, Wilbur J. *The Mind of the South*. N. Y., A. A. Knopf, 1941.

Chamberlain, Houston Stewart. *The Foundations of the Nineteenth Century, 2 Vols*. London, John Lane, 1911.

Channing, E. *History of the United States*. N. Y., Macmillan Co., 1905-32.

Commager, Henry Steele. *Documents of American History*. N. Y., F. S. Crofts & Co., 1934.

Commons, John Rogers. *A Documentary History of American Industrial Society*. Cleveland, The A. H. Clark Co., 1910.

Conrad, Earl. *Harriet Tubman*. Washington, D. C., Associated Publishers, 1943.

Conrad, Earl. *Jim Crow America*. N. Y., Duell, Sloan, & Pearce, 1947.

Cronon, Edmund David. *Black Moses: The Story of Marcus Garvey*. Madison, University of Wisconsin Press, 1955.

Curti, M. *The Growth of American Thought*. N. Y., Harper, 1951.

Davidson, Basil. *The Lost Cities of Africa*. Boston, Little, Brown and Company, 1959.

Dilke, Sir Charles Wentworth. *The Present Positions of European Politics*. London, Chapman & Hall, 1887.

Dilke, Sir Charles Wentworth. *Problems of Greater Britain*. London, Macmillan & Co., 1890.

Dorfman, Joseph. *The Economic Mind in American Civilization, 2 Vols*. N. Y., Viking Press, 1946-59.

Douglass, Frederick. *Life and Times of Frederick Douglass* (written by himself). N. Y., Pathway Press, 1941.

Du Bois, W. E. Burghardt. *The Souls of Black Folk*. Chicago, A. C. McClurg & Co., 1938.

Embree, Edwin R. *Brown America: The Story of a New Race*. N. Y., The Viking Press, 1931.

The Federalist. *Hamilton, Madison, and Jay*. N. Y., G. P. Putnam's Sons, 1891.

Fleming, Walter L. *Documentary History of Reconstruction. 2 Vols*. Cleveland, Ohio, The A. H. Clark Co., 1906-07.

Ford, H. J. *The Scotch-Irish in America.* Princeton, N. J., Princeton University Press, 1915.

Frazier, E. Franklin. *The Negro Family in the United States.* N. Y., Dryden Press, 1948.

Freyre, G. *The Masters and the Slaves.* N. Y., A. A. Knopf, 1946.

Grady, Henry W. *The New South.* N. Y., R. Bonner's Sons, 1890.

Grant, Madison. *The Passing of the Great Race.* N. Y., C. Scribner's Sons, 1921.

Hamilton, Alexander. *Alexander Hamilton and the Founding of the Nation.* (ed. Richard B. Morris) N. Y., Dial Press, 1957.

Hammond, M. B. *The Cotton Industry: An Essay in American Economic History.* London, S. Sonnenchein & Co., 1897.

Hart, A. B. *American History Told by Contemporaries.* N. Y., Macmillan Co., 1897-1929.

Helper, Hinton. *The Impending Crisis of the South: How to Meet It.* N. Y., Burdick Bros., 1860.

Herskovits, M. J. *The Myth of the Negro Past.* N. Y., Harper & Bros., 1941.

Hicks, John D. *The Populist Revolt: A History of the Farmers' Alliance and the People's Party.* Minneapolis, The University of Minnesota Press, 1931.

Jefferson, Thomas. *The Writings of Thomas Jefferson: Being His Autobiography, Correspondence, Reports, Messages, Addresses, and Other Writings Official and Private.* (ed. H. A. Washington) Washington, Taylor & Maury, 1853, 55-7.

Jenkins, William Sumner. *Pro-Slavery Thought in the Old South.* Chapel Hill, The University of North Carolina Press, 1935.

Jernegan, Marcus Wilson. *Laboring and Dependent Classes in Colonial America: 1607-1783; Studies of the Economic, Educational, and Social Significance of Slaves, Servants, Apprentices, and Poor Folk.* Chicago, Ill. The University of Chicago Press, 1931.

Kirkland, Edward C. *A History of American Economic Life.* N. Y., Appleton-Century-Crofts, 1951.

Logan, Rayford W. *The Betrayal of the Negro.* N. Y., Macmillan Co., 1954.

Madison, *Letters and Other Writings of James.* Philadelphia, J. B. Lippincott & Co., 1865.

Mangum, Charles S., Jr. *The Legal Status of the Negro.* Chapel Hill, The University of North Carolina Press, 1940.

Martineau, Harriet. *Society in America, 2 Vols.* London, Saunders & Otley, 1837.

Mazyck, Walter H. *George Washington and the Negro.* Washington, Associated Publishers, 1932.

McMaster, J. B. *History of the Peoples of the United States.* N. Y., D. Appleton & Co., 1906-13.

Miller, William. *A New History of the United States.* N. Y., Dell Publishing Co., Inc., 1958.

Monroe, *Writings of James.* (ed. S. M. Hamilton) N. Y., 1898-1903.

Moore, Richard B., *The Name 'Negro': Its Origin and Evil Use.* N. Y., Frederick Douglas Publishing Co., 1963.

Morison, S. E. *Sources and Documents Illustrating the American Revolution and the Formation of the Federal Constitution.* N. Y., Oxford University Press, 1965.

Morison, S. and Commager, H. S. *Growth of the American Republic.* N. Y., Oxford University Press, 1962.

Myers, Gustavus. *History of Bigotry in the United States.* N. Y., Random House, 1943.

Myrdal, Gunnar. *An American Dilemma: The Negro Problem and Modern Democracy.* 2 Vols. N. Y., Harper & Bros., 1944.

Nettles, Curtis P. *The Roots of American Civilization: A History of American Colonial Life.* N. Y., F. S. Crofts & Co., 1938, 1940.

Nevins, Allan. *Emergence of Modern America.* N. Y., Macmillan Co., 1927.

Palmer, R. R. *A History of the Modern World.* N. Y., Knopf, 1956.

Parrington, Vernon L. *Main Currents in American Thought.* N. Y., Harcourt, Brace & Co., 1927-30.

Phillips, Ulrich B. *The Course of the South to Secession.* (ed. E. M. Coulter) N. Y., D. Appleton-Century Co., 1939.

Quarles, Benjamin. *The Negro in the Making of America.* N. Y., Macmillan Co., 1964.

Schlesinger, A. M. and Hockett, H. C. *Political and Social Growth of the United States.* N. Y., Macmillan Co., 1933.

Schlesinger, A. W. *The Colonial Merchants and the American Revolution.* N. Y., Facsimile Library, Inc., 1939.

Simons, A. M. *Social Forces in American History.* N. Y., Macmillan Co., 1912.

Singletary, Otis A. *Negro Militia and Reconstruction.* N. Y., McGraw-Hill Book Co., 1963.

Spears, J. R. *The American Slave-Trade.* N. Y., C. Scribner's Sons, 1900.

Stoddard, Lothrop. *The Rising Tide of Color Against White World Supremacy.* N. Y., C. Scribner's Sons, 1923.

Stryker, L. P. *Andrew Johnson: A Study in Courage.* N. Y., Macmillan Co., 1929.

Turner, Frederick Jackson. *Rise of the New West, 1819-1829.* N. Y., Crowell-Collier Publishing Co., 1962.

Vance, R. B. *The South's Place in the Nation.* Washington, D. C., Public Affairs Committee, 1936.

Washington, *The Writings of George.* (ed. J. Sparks) Boston, Russell, Odiorne & Metcalf, 1834-1837.

Wertenbaker, T. J. *The Planters of Colonial Virginia.* Princeton, N. J., Princeton University Press, 1922.

Wertenbaker, T. J. *The Old South.* N. Y., C. Scribner's Sons, 1942.

Wiener, Leo. *Africa and the Discovery of America. 3 Vols.* Philadelphia, Pa., Innes & Sons, 1920-22.

Williams, Charles R. *Life of Rutherford B. Hayes. 2 Vols.* Boston, Houghton, Mifflin Co., 1914.

Williams, Eric. *Capitalism and Slavery.* Chapel Hill, N. C., University of North Carolina Press, 1944.

Woodson, Carter G. *The Negro in our History.* Washington, Associated Publishers, 1916.

Woodson, Carter G. *A History of the Negro Church,* Washington, Associated Publishers, 1921.

INDEX